P9-CFF-607

17 Cents
and a
Dream

by

Daniel Milstein

17 Cents and a Dream

Copyright © 2013 by Daniel Milstein

All rights reserved.
No part of this book may be reproduced or
transmitted in any form or by any means, electronic or
mechanical, including photocopying, recording, or by
any information storage and retrieval system, without
written permission from the author.

Library of Congress Control Number: 2013934681

ISBN: 978-0-9835527-4-1 (paperback)
ISBN: 978-0-9835527-5-8 (hardcover)
ISBN: 978-0-9835527-6-5 (eBook)

Visit our Web site at
http://DanMilstein.com
for more information.

Gold Star
PUBLISHING
A DIVISION OF GOLD STAR MORTGAGE FINANCIAL GROUP

*This book is dedicated to Julie,
my dream realized.*

Contents

The following is a true story based on the events as I recollect them. Some of the names and situations have been altered and composite characters used as well as dialogue has been created for dramatic purposes and to protect and respect the privacy of individuals

Onward
A Foreword by Mark Victor Hansen

ॐ

Everyone has heard some version of the rags to riches story, the kind that has an inherent warmth and appeal as you follow the path of individuals who overcame numerous obstacles and beat the odds to become successful in life. My friend Daniel Milstein is one of those people whose life might remind you of the protagonist in a Horatio Alger novel. The only thing that has been missing in Daniel's life is a lucky break.

Daniel didn't come across a stolen wallet that he could return to someone who would turn benefactor: he did everything himself. In his original rags to riches story, success was achieved through sheer determination and hard work regardless of the numerous hurdles that tried to break every stride he took.

Nor did Daniel have the most comfortable life in his native country of Ukraine. Growing up with few necessities and no luxuries, he and his family decided to escape the persecution that the Jews were receiving; oppression that was especially hard on his family. With a lot of effort, drive, and a little miracle, they escaped their dire situation in the USSR, armed only with the hope of finding a better life in America.

Yet it didn't get any easier for them when they landed here. Like most immigrants, Daniel didn't speak English. Their family was so broke Daniel could barely even afford to buy a banana. Yet opportunity and grace and miracles bestow us all, if only we're open to them. If there's one talent Daniel Milstein has, it's recognizing opportunities where others see challenges.

That opportunity for Daniel was working at McDonald's. Daniel had gold stars in his eyes. He knew that with enough work, persistence, and chutzpah he could do anything. He took what others may have viewed as the lowliest of low jobs, cleaning toilets, and saw it as the first stepping-stone for something better for him and his family.

In the way people tend to do, his coworkers teased him and ridiculed him. The taunts he was subjected to would have broken anyone's will, but not Daniel. He used the ridicule as inspiration and motivation.

The first hurdle that Daniel had to overcome was the language barrier. For a man who had a life like a bed of thorns, this would have been a Herculean task if there ever was one. But he did it. Daniel had sheer willpower and inspirational desperation.

The spiritual language has a saying, "seek and you shall find." The concept is simple and straightforward. Once you've decided that you want to achieve something, everything around you will work to get it for you as long as you remain dedicated. This was what worked for Daniel.

I've been writing my whole life, working on how to grow rich in a niche. When Daniel saw a niche, first by helping other immigrants, he jumped at the opportunity to help others. My parents were Danish immigrants, and I know first-hand the challenges they faced. But Daniel didn't see them as challenges. He said, "What I'm going to do is help the people that nobody else is helping."

Over the years Daniel has become the No.1 mortgage loan officer in the world, and has built one of the fastest-growing companies in the United States.

So what you have here is a guy who came from nowhere. He overcame the toughest of obstacles that would have pulled anyone down. He saw what he liked, decided what he wanted, and went after it until the world around him had to bend to his will so that he could get what he wanted and, through hard work, what he deserved.

Through pure determination, fortitude, and attitude Daniel pulled out of impossibly difficult situations. His story is true. His story is a personal inspiration to me, and I hope it will inspire you too and help maximize your potential so you may aim for the greatest of dreams.

Prologue
My American Dream

❧

The wide bay window looks out onto a city brimming with both the promise of future possibilities and the pain of past failures. I spin my chair around just long enough to see the sun set. The colors span across city blocks, stretching shadows long on top of the many buildings that failed to survive the worst financial meltdown since the Great Depression.

I tilt my chair back and wrap my hands around the back of my neck as I scan the narrowed streets filled with cars and people, here and there, the remnants of the businesses that are no more. The bank on the corner went under. The mortgage firm down the road tanked. And all I can think about is the path I started on so many years ago that put me in this very chair today. Like a man caught beneath a rain of falling bombs, I not only dodged the devastation of the failing economy, I ducked my head, pulled at the wrists of those at my side, and ran past the falling debris of financial ruin. To survive, I sacrificed basic human needs, such as food and sleep, while many others in the financial industry were not so fortunate, and there are now silent brick and mortar buildings bearing the cold testament to their failure.

The phone on my desk rings and I am startled out of my daydream.

As the call has been answered at the front desk, I look into the distance and remember a time when all that inspired me were the Golden Arches high above McDonald's. My American dream began long before stepping foot onto American soil, but McDonald's was the place where my idea of everything about what America represented began. It was my chance to become whoever I wanted to be. As my grandfather always taught me, America was the place where I was allowed to dream big dreams, because anything could happen if I just worked hard enough.

Long after my years in the Ann Arbor fast food restaurant, an experience that gave me, a non-English speaking immigrant, his first op-portunity, the owner of that same store purchased the land directly next to mine to build his multi-million dollar home. And even now, with the many blessings I've received, I look back and remember these feelings of opportunity and hope for a better life for my parents, brother, grandmother, and for myself.

Life has become more than I ever could have imagined it to be when I was a small boy in Kiev. I didn't dare to dream about becoming a best-selling author or being appointed to serve on many boards, including my Alma Mater, or more importantly becoming one of the youngest CEOs of all time in a business that started out of a closet with my savings of $3,000.

As the colors of the sun streak through the window, I think all these things can happen only in America. Because of my parents' sacrifice all those years back, I am now able to give my daughter Julie all the things every parent wants for their child. She will know that dreams can come true, that she never needs to live in fear of prejudice, and that she will never go hungry. She will never be homeless, and she will never go a single day without the undying love of her father.

I pick up the silver picture frame that sits on my desk and look at the gentle brown eyes of my sweet little girl, my finger tracing the outer edge of the frame as I smile right back at her free-spirited grin. I thank God for that grin, and I hope that she never loses it. I feel a twinge of pride in my chest at the thought that as long as I live, my Julie will never go a moment without feeling loved, protected, and cherished.

Through all those sleepless nights, working 23 hours a day, I did everything in my power to make one thing clear: Julie comes first. My only hope is that someday, when she's old enough to know all that I've done in my life and everything I am, she will never need to wonder where she stood in my list of priorities.

She will already know.

"You have a call on line one," I hear through the phone's speaker.

I snap out of my reverie, set the frame back in its place, and revert back to business. But when I pick up the phone, I have no idea what's about to come through from the other end. As I listen, I try to catch my breath, to let what I'm hearing sink in, and to realize that this is the culmination of everything I've endured and all that has come to be. When I slept on a beanbag chair in a 335-square foot apartment with five others, surviving the Chernobyl catastrophe, I could never have imagined that this is where I'd be today.

I hang up the phone, spin my chair back towards the sunlight that is now melting into the sky, and smile. It's a phone call from *Inc.* magazine, telling me that we have been named to the *Inc.* 500 list of America's fastest-growing companies. My American Dream is no longer just a dream.

It's my life.

I - Chernobyl:
The 1986 Secret Disaster

ॐॐ

In the predawn hours of Saturday, April 26, 1986, a worker conducting a routine systems test at the Chernobyl Nuclear Power Plant pushed a button to initiate an emergency core shutdown. Seconds later, an explosion ripped through Reactor Number Four, blasting a deadly plume of radioactive material hundreds of feet into the atmosphere.

At that moment, 78 miles away in the Ukrainian city of Kiev, I was sleeping peacefully in my family's apartment, sharing a pullout couch with my three-year-old brother, Alex. I was ten years old and blissfully unaware that we were literally in the shadow of the worst nuclear power plant disaster in history.

That pullout bed was a luxury to me. I had been assigned to sleep in a beanbag chair until my grandmother, my dad's mother, made it to the top of a fifteen year waiting list and moved into her own place. Now that she was no longer living with us, our 335-square foot apartment seemed spacious with just my parents, Alex, and myself living there. We were a close family, and part of me missed having my grandmother around, but sleeping in a bed more than made up for my loss.

My personal hero was my grandfather, Dr. Joseph Khiterer, who worked as a dentist at the nearby Military Aviation Engineering Academy. He was a gentle, moderate, unassuming man who could instantly transform my day from dreary to magnificent with nothing more than a smile and a pat on the head. When he spoke, his words were profound, and when he smiled the corners of his eyes would crinkle with kindness.

He was also the family photojournalist. He was the proud owner of a fine Russian-built Zenit camera that always seemed to be at hand, always seemed to be aimed at his family and documenting our lives. Ironically, since he was the photographer, he was rarely included in the photographs.

One of my earliest memories as a very young child is of my grandfather sitting across the table, watching me attack an omelet.

"You must always remember," he said to me, "that you only have two things in this world: your name and your reputation. Also know that you can be anything or anybody you want to be. But don't expect that anyone is going to do this for you. Not your parents, not me. You will become exactly who you yourself work to become – nothing more and nothing less."

"Really? I could be anything?"

"Anything."

"Even a great doctor like you?"

He smiled and shook his head. "I am certain that you will be far greater than me."

As I grew into a boy, my grandfather would often tell me about a country where I could have the chance to make something more of myself than the local party leaders would force me to be. "Someday we will all go to this place where dreams can come true. We will go to America."

For years I thought every day about what it would be like if my family could go to this wonderful place, America, but I also knew that there were obstacles in our way. I may have actually been dreaming about this land of opportunity on that fateful morning in 1986.

In the days after the explosion at Chernobyl, the government told us nothing about what was happening. One afternoon I stepped over to the small window, lifted the curtain, and looked to the street to see men wearing white, alien-looking masks and rubber suits, scrubbing the ground clean. The men moved slowly in their heavy uniforms under a blackened cloud that covered the city. They gathered along the side of the road, in front of the other five-story building that looked exactly like mine, but no matter how long or hard they scrubbed, they couldn't erase the lingering smell of the cinders floating to the ground.

I closed my eyes and opened them again, my heart pounding in my chest, and looked down at the potatoes I'd just planted in the window box. The dirt was in a loose mound, my fingerprints still visible. My throat clutched tight as I tried to conjure up a normal breath, while the sight of those ghost-like masks seared through me.

Sweating and lightheaded, I thought about running into the bathroom, a room so small that we had to turn sideways to get into it, to compose myself. Instead, I let the curtain drop, collapsed onto my bed, and flipped on the television to check all three channels for Tchaikovsky's *Swan Lake. Swan Lake* on the state-controlled TV was a sure sign that something bad had happened, like the death of a president or something equally monumental. Beyond the plume of smoke that sprinkled ash over our streets, we had no idea what had happened to our beautiful city.

Through the murky haze, a crowd of confused people began to panic, running rampant through ashes and embers, and we locked the door against the threat of the mob. I could hear my parents whispering, making plans of how to handle this situation, as I sat and comforted my three-year-old little brother, Alex.

In the days after April 26, the foreign radio airwaves were fiercely guarded by the KGB, and no matter how hard my father tried, it was nearly impossible to piece together the facts in the face of all the propaganda streaming through. That propaganda was still working fine on the day of the annual May parade, when millions of people, including children, were forced to walk the streets breathing air that was thick with a lingering, deadly fog.

My father was finally fed up. He wanted answers, and he was going to get them no matter what had to be done. In typical engineer fashion, he constructed super antennae to break through the electronic barriers put in place by the government. He carefully installed them in just the right spots and wriggled each one until noise poured through. At first there was only static. He twisted the knobs delicately back and forth until he found the perfect notch, and a voice from the Western World came streaming through the speakers.

We all gathered around to listen, breathing in unison. I leaned in, straining to hear the announcer's words. My pulse quickened and I could see Alex's big eyes darting from face to face, trying to understand what we were doing. I knew it was going to be big news by the way my parents looked nervously at one another, and I could feel my hair stand on end.

Even with my father's antennae, the broadcast was choppy and static-laden, but once it came through we heard more than we could have prepared for.

"Swedish workers had radioactive particles on their clothes that were traced back to the Chernobyl power plant," the broadcaster announced.

I stared at the radio, thinking, *We are a lot closer to Chernobyl than Sweden is!*

Two weeks after the incident the government began to fully realize the horror of the power plant explosion, but by then a nearly unimaginable human tragedy was in the making. Birds with two heads, malformed infants, and the quickly rising number of people sickened and dying were overwhelming Chernobyl and surrounding areas. There were thousands of people exposed to harmful doses of radiation, and at least 100,000 others who would succumb to some type of cancer decades after the fact. School was immediately closed and orders were sent for school-aged children to stay home until they could be evacuated to the Black Sea.

Through all the chaos, and with all of us battling an overwhelming sense of fear, it took an additional three weeks to organize camps and transportation for the terrified children. Train tickets had been sold out months in advance while the government prepared for the evacuation, which meant that unless we were going on one of those buses, my parents had to figure out some other way to get us to safety.

One by one, groups of 40 or more children said their last goodbyes to their parents and waved to them from the bus windows. My grandmother, like many other survivors of the Holocaust, had tears in her eyes, no doubt remembering other trains rolling away, and the pain of never being reunited with some of her family again. Children as young as age five were hauled off, onto a bus, with no way of knowing if they would ever see their parents, who were to stay behind for work, again. Other families adopted many children because, sadly, their parents, who had been left behind, died from a combination of heartbreak and radiation.

I wondered what would happen to us. Would the food still be safe to eat? Would there even be any food left with everything in ruins? How would we get through the roads? Were there any roads left? Would my brother and I be okay? I tried to stay strong, but I could feel my legs shaking at the thought of the possible answers to those burning questions. We heard of families barricading themselves inside their homes, while others tried to flee. What would we do?

Almost immediately after the accident, the government had sent all the medical professionals they could find, including my grandfather, to Chernobyl to treat nearby residents. None of these people knew that the radiation level around the plant was 100 times that of the atomic bombs dropped on Hiroshima and Nagasaki combined.

It could not have been long though before my grandfather and his colleagues realized that the people they were treating were suffering from severe radiation poisoning. Their training must have also have told them that by sending them into Chernobyl, the government had effectively sentenced the medical teams themselves to a slow, painful death. By New Years Eve, 1988, the invisible poison had done its work and destroyed nearly every organ in my grandfather's body.

In the USSR, New Year's Eve was by far the biggest holiday of the year. Since we weren't allowed to celebrate any religious holidays, we were obliged to cram as much revelry as we possibly could into the last day of the year. Ded Moroz, the Russian version of Santa Claus, made his appearance on December 31, and most homes had a Yolka, or New Year's tree, that looked remarkably similar to western Christmas trees.

We didn't have a Yolka in our house that year though. My mother, my father, my grandmother, my brother, and I all sat in our apartment, waiting for word from the hospital that my grandfather had left this world. I was too numb to talk or even to cry as I stared at, without seeing, the images flickering on the television and listened to the joyful fireworks exploding over the city.

At 4:00 a.m. the phone rang. My mother listened for a few moments without speaking, then slowly hung up the phone and turned to us. "Your grandfather is gone."

I was twelve years old, and far too manly to show my emotions, especially in front of the women. I bit my lip hard as I pushed my chair back, walked across the apartment, and crawled into the pullout bed where Alex was already sleeping. Then I buried my face in my pillow and tried not to shake him awake with my sobs.

A couple of days later I found myself standing dazed in my grandfather's house among a room full of people. Through the window, almost next door, I could see the Aviation Academy. My grandfather, wearing his best suit, seemed to be sleeping in a coffin at the end of the room. Everybody was crying.

A soldier with tears in his eyes came up to me and shook my hand. "He was a great man," said the soldier. "You must be Daniel."

I nodded.

"It's as if I already know you. Your grandfather talked about you all the time. He said that you are going to be an important man someday."

I nodded again.

He shook my hand once more. "I am sorry for your loss," he said and then he stood awkwardly at attention, saluted me, and melted back into the crowd.

This happened over and over again, so many times that I lost count.

"... You must be Daniel..."

"... Told me so much about you..."

"... He was very proud of you..."

I was surprised at the incredible number of lives my grandfather had touched, and was stunned at how many strangers he had apparently regaled with tales of his amazing and talented grandson, Daniel.

My only other clear memory of that day was my grandmother taking me by the shoulder and leading me to the kitchen, where we sat together at the table. "I have something for you," she said. She reached into a small bag, pulled out my grandfather's camera, and handed it to me. "He wanted you to have this. He told me that he wanted you to someday take lots of pictures of his great grandchildren."

I took the camera in my hands and looked back toward the man at rest in the other room. "Thank you," I whispered.

II - Behind Closed Doors

~∞~

My parents refused to just let us die. During the years after the Chernobyl accident, the radiation also claimed the life of my paternal grandmother and it would be the source of my father's many health issues for years to come. In fact, it seemed as though nearly everyone we knew became ill at some point.

I began to wonder if I had been contaminated and the thought was crippling. For all I knew, I could be walking around like a ticking time bomb and everything my grandfather dreamed of was destined to die along with him.

They assured me that we were going to be fine. They said that everything would be okay. They had always been so courageous that I had no reason to believe otherwise. Even at the tender age of ten, I trusted them fully. They wouldn't let me leave the apartment until they could make plans for Alex and me to go to Moscow. They said they couldn't let us go to the Black Sea camps where all the other children went, because they were under-staffed and overcrowded. They made the sacrifice because they wanted us safe. Until it was time to leave, we were to remain behind the door and away from whatever danger was outside of it.

Of course, like other adults, my parents were forced to continue working, which meant that they had to go outside and walk around amongst the radioactive ash and polluted air, pretending that life was normal.

Twenty days passed in the stuffy little apartment. Alex and I were more than ready to go to Moscow for the next four months. My parents planned to take alternate vacations to stay with us, so we'd never be alone. Meanwhile, they remained in Kiev like all the other parents, and hoped that the radiation wouldn't find its way into their lungs. This wasn't easy because we couldn't all just leave. Cars were a luxury most people just didn't have then. Traveling to Moscow wasn't just challenging; it was a completely life changing ordeal.

There would be no more soccer outside our apartment, no more guitar playing in the hallway, and no more of the clear skies I had always taken for granted. Things were going to be different in a big way, but I had no way of knowing just how different until the proverbial dust settled.

The grocery shelves were bare and the food that was left didn't have price tags. Instead, it had radiation levels. My dad measured radiation with a device he handmade and kept on him at all times. It was similar to the meter a photographer would use to measure light. My grandfather had made one too; they were both electrically inclined and highly motivated to keep us safe.

Even as we started on our way to Moscow, the truth about the Chernobyl accident wasn't enough anymore. I wondered what would happen to us in the future; if we would stay safe or if we would always have fear on our shoulders. If it weren't Chernobyl, would it always be something?

Once we were away from Kiev, I often wandered the streets of Moscow in a crowd of nine million crazed people, hoping for food, for human contact, for solace. My parents and I would take turns searching for food throughout the shortage. When they'd go, I'd watch Alex and my four-year-old little cousin and vice versa. It was a family effort to find food for us not only to thrive, but also to survive.

I'd take whatever means of transportation I could find, jumping on the 6:00 a.m. subway train

and changing to another to find my way to the
Red Square. That's where I'd wait in line seven or
eight hours to see Lenin's Tomb, while Alex stayed
home with my mother or father. Then I'd wander
through herds of bustling people, stuff my hands
in my pockets, and wait in the four to six-hour
grocery lines and think about what I would do if I
were already sick and didn't know it. Would I feel
it? Would it hurt? I thought about what would
happen if I died. I thought about my apartment
in Kiev and how I'd have given anything to sleep
in that beanbag chair with my brother again. I
wanted everything to go back to normal.

I was deep in thought and left to my own
devices most of the time, so I'd meander through
the stunning Kremlin area and look out over the
river, daydreaming about all the things I wanted to
be, all the things Grandpa said I could be. I loved
to walk to the Red Square and weave in and out
of the cars, paying no attention to the time of day
or how long I'd been walking. I just wanted to be
out in the fresh air, breathing life into my lungs. It
seemed like children matured more quickly in Rus-
sia, and even at ten I always felt and was treated
much older. It wasn't an issue for kids like me to
walk around for hours on end with no supervi-
sion. I often looked around at everything Moscow
had to offer. Among other things, the breathtaking

churches, churches in which no services were ever allowed, always caught my eye. And while many of these sites were lovely, I missed Kiev and the life I had before.

I missed my home.

In late August, months after the citywide evacuation, the USSR ordered all the children back to school. We returned to Kiev and our small apartment, which seemed even smaller after having been gone, but things didn't feel the way they were before. Life was as normal as it could be, all things considered. It felt both good and bad to walk through the slim doorframe, but I wasn't sure if I could ever feel safe again. Everyone who was still alive seemed to have bonded over what had happened, but we were all afraid to go to the market, not knowing what was contaminated, even with my father's radiation detector. It was so many of those things I'd never thought much about before, that I'd have to really pay attention to from then on.

Each time the moon rose and the sun fell over the Kiev Sea, so close to Chernobyl, it would light up the sky with its contaminated waters. The waves would dance and crash like glowing ribbons, intertwined. And those freshly planted potatoes I'd left in May were still there too. The radiation that lingered sank into the roots and fed the plants, causing them to grow to the size of watermelons. It was just another reminder of how Chernobyl would impact every last particle of that chapter of my life and many chapters to come.

III - Night of a Thousand Fears

ὓ⁓Ὑ

"Shhh," my father scolded my brother, sitting next to him on the bed and covering his mouth.

We could hear the creak of someone coming upstairs. I was a teenager at that time and too macho to show my fear, but I was having a hard time keeping up the facade. My hand felt for the knife I'd hidden under my pillow, to make sure it was still there. There had been graffiti scribbled all over the outside of our walls for weeks. My father had tried to scrub it clean, but remnants of the hateful words remained.

They were coming to kill us. We knew that for sure.

If it hadn't been for the sound of my own heart pounding in my ears, I might have heard my father's dry swallow, his eyes scanning back and forth, as alert as an animal that knows that the hunter is near.

My father had a sixth sense when it came to protecting his family. Several times before, someone had thrown rocks through our front window; he always seemed to know what was about to happen.

"Get down!" he yelled, ripping my shirt collar and dragging me to the floor. The stones with anti-Semitic phrases and pictures drawn all over them shattered the glass and fell just inches from our heads. We wondered if it would ever end, or if we'd have to endure this fear forever.

His ears perked as he listened to what sounded like someone walking up the stairs, and only after minutes of intense concentration, did he finally loosen his grip on my brother's mouth and heave a sigh of relief.

I watched the sweat glisten on my father's forehead and roll down the side of his face. "Don't say a word," he finally whispered barely loud enough for us to hear.

My mother sat up straight in her bed, doing everything in her power to hold back the tears, being strong for all of us, but every creak and crack made her jump.

Tonight was the night. They wanted us to die.

It wasn't the first time we'd experienced anti-Semitic hatred, but it was the first night I could remember that was actually called "Kill the Jews" night. Although I was barely a teenager, I knew what was going on, even if my parents didn't want to talk about it. It had been all over the neighborhood that week; the Jew-haters had assembled a mob that was hell-bent on "cleansing" Kiev of us. They needed someone to blame for all the political arrests, the poverty, and the crime.

This was chillingly familiar to the Jews of Kiev. During two days in September 1941, the Nazis occupying the city took more than 37,000 Jews to a ravine in the northwestern section of Kiev called Babi Yar. There they were made to leave all their belongings behind, disrobe, and march to the edge of the gorge in groups of 10, where the Nazis shot them down with machine guns. This was to punish them for the "crime" of being Jews. Over the next few months the Nazis executed Gypsies, mental patients, prisoners of war, and other civilians at Babi Yar so that by the end of 1941 the bodies of more than 100,000 innocent victims lay at the bottom of that gorge.

My immediate family was fortunately not in Kiev during the Babi Yar massacres. Both of my grandmothers and my grandfather Khiterer had been evacuated to Siberia, where they supported the war effort by working long days in Soviet factories. One of my grandmothers was so tiny that she had to stand on a stool just to reach the controls of the machine she was operating.

Many of our other relatives were not lucky enough to have been relocated, and perished at the hands of the Nazis at Babi Yar.

Despite the fact that Jews were not treated particularly well in much of Soviet society, my paternal grandfather fought with the Russian army in Stalingrad, where he was wounded and lost his sight. This was particularly ironic, since before the war he had been an artist, a painter by profession. Later, when surgeons restored his sight, his first act was to paint a patriotic portrait of Joseph Stalin.

Like my grandfather, I loved my country, but as that night went on we all began to wonder how long we could survive. How long could we go on struggling day after day? How long could we be ridiculed and treated like second-class citizens, not knowing if we would be accused of a petty crime and locked up for a lifetime? How long could we feel trapped, knowing that there had to be something better in store for us, but never given a glimpse of the possibilities?

Kill the Jews night was life-changing for all of us. It was the culmination of all our daily struggles up to that point. We could no longer just ignore those struggles as "life." This was not normal, this was not acceptable, and I think something finally clicked with my parents. They knew we had to find a better way. My parents were simple people, but desperation either breaks you or makes you stronger. It amplifies the person you really are inside, and only time would tell what it would do for each of us.

Others like us were hiding too, in hopes that a non-Jewish friend would help them. But it was rare that anyone would voluntarily get involved and put their own life at risk when they didn't have to. I later found out that one of my mother's friends had offered to help, but everyone else had turned a blind eye.

If there is one thing about my parents that I now understand, it is that cowardice is not in their DNA. They were the descendants of survivors who had undergone far worse than what we were going through now, and they had raised their children to survive as well.

They had undergone threats of the Holocaust, severe winters, starvation, and war. They wanted something better for their children and their children's children, and although I may not have been able to appreciate it then, my parents found the courage in their hearts to protect what little they had.

In addition to their bravery, they had integrity, and they persevered no matter what. My father would have done anything to protect his family that night, even if that meant wiring the door with over 200 watts of electricity, which he did. Even though he was an electrical engineer, I still don't know how he came up with the wires and connectors to do it. Much like food, electronic supplies were scarce. My father was incredibly resourceful when it came to keeping us safe.

I think I gained more respect for my parents that night than I ever had before. My mom and dad were fighters, quiet warriors. They would have defended us to their very last breath.

We could hear the shouting from the streets, the venomous rants, and the hatred; "Kill the Jews!" they yelled. They were getting closer. I didn't know if we were going to make it out alive that night, but I knew one thing for sure: we had to get out of there.

IV - Picking Up the Pieces

༺჻༻

"Wake up," a voice said. My eyes sprung open, trying to focus on the face in front of me. Where was I? Where was my family? Were they still alive?

I felt a surge of panic in my heart at the thought, until I rubbed my eyes and realized that it was my dad. "You're going to be late for school."

What? That didn't make sense; we had the afternoon shift at school. And then I realized how late it was. Neither my mom nor my dad had gone to work that morning, as they were understandably still in shock over the night's events. There was silence in our home, except for the sizzling sound of my mother's cooking. As comforting as that familiar sound was, fear still lingered in the air like a bad odor.

We had survived that night somehow. I patted my chest. I was alive.

My mom was already ordering us to pick up around our apartment and make the bed. My dad had unwired the electrical lines from the door. We didn't say much to each other that morning, though I remember my mom mumbling something about how worried she was about us going school alone. My dad assured her that he would get us there in one piece.

Truth be told, we didn't know what was going on outside our door, or if there were people waiting for us. No one knew.

My brother was filled with questions, which he rattled off, as usual, to no avail. Eventually he discovered that no one was going to answer any of his questions, so he might as well not say anything at all.

We stepped out the door, walking down the steps as if we were about to step into a war zone. My father rushed ahead of us. "Come on, let's get going," he instructed.

My breath was ragged, as I saw in the streets the remnants of the night before; broken glass, what was left of picket signs, ashes from some of the fires they had caused, and vodka bottles. It wasn't pretty.

I saw the ragged scraps of a sign with derogatory anti-Semitic words written on it.

"What's that?" my brother asked my dad.

My father just cleared his throat, took him by the hand, and said, "Trash."

My brother didn't understand what it meant, but I did. To have what seems like the whole world hate you, because of where you were born or what blood ran through your veins was almost unbearable. It would take me years to overcome the pain and even today, when I hear such horrible words, they still sting.

"But why?" my brother asked him. "Why do they hate us?"

"Because," my father said, trying to put it delicately as he thought about how to phrase it. "Because we're different, and they need someone to blame."

"For what?" my brother asked.

"For things being the way they are; things could be better."

"But why is that our fault?" he asked.

My father took a long breath and stopped at a street corner. He looked out over the city's beautiful skyline where the sun met the earth. The domes of the church sparkled with golden brilliance, reflecting off the cobblestone streets. In the distance we could see the subway where people hustled and bustled, getting on with their busy lives. To the left, the park was trimmed with lush, full trees and thick flowers blooming throughout. To the right were massive buildings built centuries ago; breathtaking monstrosities, a testament to a country once great but now crumbling from political instability.

But the most stunning view of the whole city was that of the Motherland Monument. She stood tall atop the museum, her shiny sword and shield aimed up high into the air. She gave me hope. She gave us all hope. When the sun hit her just right, she didn't just shine, she glowed.

My father squinted at the landmarks of our beautiful city, our Kiev. "You see that?" he pointed to a theater way in the distance. My brother shielded his eyes from the sun, as my dad lifted him to get a better look.

"Yeah?" he answered.

"And that?" my dad pointed to another building. "That's ours."

"Ours?"

"Our people built that. We are just as much a part of this city as anybody else and don't you forget it. This stone, and this sidewalk, that building and that one, our grandparents and their grandparents put their souls into all of it. This city was built on our backs and with our brains. You be proud of where you come from. Never be ashamed – not ever."

It had been a while since I'd seen my dad that serious, and quite frankly a long time since my dad had said that much at one time. But when he did speak, it was meaningful. I thought about what he had said. It gave me a sense of pride, and I felt a little bit better than I had before.

We walked a few blocks before we began to realize that no one was going to come out and get us, though I stayed tense all the way to school and throughout the day. It didn't help that I had to attend a military prep course with a retired Colonel who threatened me daily with ethnic slurs and promises that someone like me could only be good for one thing: cleaning toilets.

Times like this provided the driving force behind my parents' efforts to get us out of there. It is difficult looking back on those days, and I have buried much of the pain beneath new and more pleasant memories. But those moments, stuck in time, will always stay with me. They're my history and part of my DNA. They became my motivations to succeed.

The people trying to hunt us down may have terrified us that night, but they also sparked something in all of us, something they could never drive out: the desire for a better life.

V - The Dream

❧

My alarm rang at 4:00 a.m. and I jumped out of bed. I had the notion that I could make money to help out the family, by being first in line to get supplies from the neighborhood stores before they reached their allotted number of products for the day. Because items such as milk and sugar were scarce, the stores would only have so many to sell, so that even with a coupon, being able to buy what you wanted was never guaranteed.

I quietly left the apartment and met a couple of friends at the store to purchase whatever we could, but we had no intention of keeping any of it. Instead, we waited patiently until 8:00 a.m. and sold the goods at a profit on the "black market." We were ignorant of the possible consequences, such as being caught by the authorities or worse, the Russian, Armenian, and Chechnyan mafias.

On the other hand, this could have been the start of my budding entrepreneurial skills.

After we sold out of products, I hurried home. Between my school schedule and illegal black market activities, I didn't have a lot of free time. I'd usually fill my days playing soccer in the summer and ice hockey in the winter. If I wasn't doing these things or doing homework, I was probably taking care of my little brother.

Later that morning, after I slid into the apartment and quietly went back to bed, I was awakened by the sound of the front door lock being twisted in the rotted wood. I could hear creaking footsteps moving from room to room. As far as I knew, my brother and I were alone in the apartment. I sat up in bed, the sheet falling to my waist, and listened. I took a big gulp and knotted the sheet between my knuckles as the footsteps grew closer and closer.

I tried not to move.

I held my breath, and my heart pounded as I watched the doorknob slowly turn and the door ease open. My mother and father, who should have been at work, poked their heads into the room and tip-toed to my bedside, careful not to wake Alex. They knelt down beside me.

"What's the matter?" I asked.

My mother took a long, deep breath and looked to my father, who was silent. He looked right at me with eyes very much like my own.

For some reason, looking into his eyes at that moment reminded me of the amusement park he'd frequently take me to. It was the manual go-carts I loved most. He would push me for hours until it was time for our favorite barbeque shish kebobs. This memory came from nowhere, but I welcomed it and embraced it.

"It's time for us to make official plans now," he said, bringing me back to reality.

"Plans? For what," I asked.

Mother wrapped her hand around mine and leaned in close. "To go to America."

"America!" Alex shot up out of bed in an excited frenzy. The smile on his face was dripping with anticipation. "We're going to America!"

"Shhh! Quiet!" My father said, cupping his hand around Alex's mouth. "You cannot repeat this to anyone."

I couldn't restrain my smile, but I also couldn't find the right words. "Why now?"

My mother's lip quivered, and her eyes grew moist. "I can't let my boys become part of the Soviet Army. We must leave before it's too late.

In America, you can be a doctor. You can become something. Here, I fear you and your brother will become nothing. "

"No one thinks I'll be a doctor," I said. "They say I'll only be a mechanic, that I'm not smart enough to do anything else. They all say this, even the teachers."

Mother put a finger to my lips and gently shushed me. "That is nonsense. People told Thomas Edison he wasn't smart enough, and look what he accomplished. You will be a doctor. But not here."

Alex collapsed onto the pullout and twisted the sheet around his legs, kicking and flailing the way small children do. He was restless the way we all were in the USSR. He just didn't completely understand what it meant. At the time, I'm not sure I completely understood what it meant. I only knew of all the things my grandfather and parents had told me about a better life in America. But Kiev was home.

"There's another family that's going to leave too. I've been talking with them about our decision. They're going to keep our secret, and we will keep theirs. They'll be leaving sooner than us, though, and the whole process will take quite a bit of time."

My father vigorously rubbed and pinched the

skin between his eyes and then lifted his head to meet our curious stares. "Listen to me. You cannot tell anyone. Not a single soul. Doing so may mean our jobs, jail time, losing our home, and much worse."

"What's worse than all that?" I asked, quietly.

My parents looked at one another with a sense of fear lingering between them.

"Death."

Alex and I sat in silence. The only sound in the room was that of our breathing.

"You understand?" my father asked.

Alex and I nodded. My mother patted my hand once more, and then stood to leave with my father. "Have a good day at school, and remember, say nothing of what we just discussed."

They closed the door closed behind them and their footsteps creaked through and back out of the apartment. Only two seconds passed before Alex started in. "What's America like?"

I lowered my head to the pillow with my hands locked behind me. "It's where I'm going to become a dentist and drive a car like Grandpa. It's where good things happen."

"What does America look like?" Alex asked.

I leaned in to him, the way our father would have, and lowered my voice to a whisper. "You can't say these things in front of anyone but me. Do you understand that?"

His eyes fell.

"This is serious Alex. It will only bring bad things if you talk about it. This is our secret."

He nodded, but I wasn't really sure that he grasped the danger we'd be in if he accidentally slipped.

"Okay," I said. "No more questions. Go get dressed."

I walked through the tiny apartment and opened the door. On the stoop laid a rolled-up newspaper, resting against a brick. I un-twisted the rubber band and unfolded the paper. The front page was dominated by the word "TRAI-TOR" in bold black print. Beneath this stark headline was a picture depicting the public ridi-cule of some people who had surrendered their passports. Balled up fists and angry faces sur-rounded the humiliated parties.

They were being shamed for trying to find new jobs, to make a new start. They were trying to flee, just as my family was planning. In retribu-tion, the government had taken away their work permits, without which there would be no jobs and no future for them.

I wondered if that's what would become of us. I rubbed at the headline on that paper so hard that the ink smeared onto my fingers. I didn't read the rest of the story. I'd seen enough. I knew that leaving for America would be dangerous, but it was hard to grasp how dangerous or what it would mean for my family and me.

During school that afternoon, the teacher sat me down to go over a test I had taken. When she first called me up I thought that maybe she'd somehow heard of the conversation I'd had with my parents. I thought I was in trouble and my family was in danger.

Instead, I could see that the letter at the top of the sheet was a "C," while there were no red marks anywhere on the white paper. "Why did I receive a 'C'?" I asked. "I didn't get anything wrong."

She pushed the paper towards me. "I already gave all the good grades I was allowed. Maybe next time..."

She nodded me back to my seat and I carried that "C" with my head hung low. My mother always taught me to work five times harder than everyone else since, "Just because you are Jewish, it will always be an uphill battle."

Somehow, I managed to get through school that day without saying a single word, even though thoughts were racing through my mind. I had started to understand the opportunity that awaited us, and I wanted so badly to set foot onto the land of dreams that I could almost taste it. I knew, despite what everyone else had been saying about me, that I really could be something there. All through class my legs shook, as I thought about Alex, and who he might have told, and the danger that he may have put us in.

I rushed to his school to get him and together we ran home and locked the door behind us. He was still full of questions, but my mind kept wandering back to that newspaper. Even though my parents weren't part of the Communist party, would we be humiliated too? I imagined standing in the center of town, high up on that stage, with everyone condemning us, banishing us from the USSR, but keeping us from America by denying us our passports and visas. Where would we go? Would we have any home at all?

The thoughts were, quite literally, paralyzing.

That afternoon I kept myself busy with chores. I gathered and carried a reeking bag of trash down five flights of stairs. Even though I didn't enjoy it, this sort of work taught me the discipline I needed. Today, even though I have a maid, I still make my own bed every morning, and I am partial to any activities that involve household cleaning.

For some reason, at that moment, when I reached the bottom of the staircase, I heard my grandfather's voice in my ear. "You have to get to

America, Dan," he said. "But don't tell anyone. It's our secret."

I dropped the trash and stood for a moment, looking to the sky. I didn't hear anything, but the breeze swirling past our building. I heaved a sigh, walked back up the five flights, and waited for my parents to get home.

Once inside, I collapsed on the couch and dreamed about the days at summer camp when I was small, a privilege my grandparents had earned for me. And I dreamed of later times, when I crawled inside huge cast iron pots and scraped the burnt milk from the sides. Then I was a dish-washer working long hours at the camp for little pay, and I peeled potatoes for over 200 kids every single day. I didn't do it because I had to. I did it because I wanted to.

My parents instilled a great work ethic in me from the start. I was taught to be self-sufficient, to take care of myself, and to help others, which is why I never minded being there for Alex while my parents worked. In my free time, I loved to journey with him through the woods to pick wild strawberries. At night we'd sing over a bonfire. Those wonderful memories carried me through some of my most difficult days.

When my mother arrived home, she had tears streaming down her face. Did someone tell on us?

Silently sobbing, she lifted a newspaper from her bag and set it on the table.

I didn't say a word. I just pulled up a chair and waited for her to speak.

She poked a finger at the picture in the paper I'd seen earlier that day. "These are the people."

I swallowed what felt like a prickly ball the size of the moon. "What people?"

She sniffled. "The family I told you about. They were going to leave and someone found out and reported them. Now look."

I glanced over at Alex who was quiet, resting on the couch.

"What's going to happen to them?"

"The government will make them disappear."

"But how can they?"

"You give up your apartment and resign from the Communist party. If they find out you're going to leave, that we're going to leave, they'll say we did something, something bad, like stealing. Then they torture you until you can't take it anymore, until you say you did whatever they claimed, so they can throw you in jail and prosecute you, and then you can never, ever leave."

She pushed the paper towards me. The look in her eyes urged me to read on, but the faces of that family stopped me cold. It could be us standing in that square, surrounded by enemies. If anyone found out that we wanted to leave, it would be us.

At the end of the week, we entered the United States government office as frightened as could be. We had no idea what would be involved in actually getting us to the land of our dreams. When they led us into the small, stuffy office, we remained silent. Two men, serious and official looking, entered the room and asked us question after question. The process took a lot of time, and I worked hard to remain patient. The more interviews we had, the more it began to dawn on me that I would be leaving the only home I'd ever known. It was starting to feel real, and at the same time it felt as if it was never actually going to really happen.

As we left, I looked at my mother. She didn't say much as she strode down the hallway to the exit, but her eyes had filled with tears. My father looked ahead at the horizon and then to her, grabbing hold of her hand. It was hard to put my feelings into words, to sort out everything that was happening, but I knew it was the start of things to come, good or bad.

I looked to Alex, and I knew that the only way we could escape without getting caught depended on him keeping quiet. But how long could he really keep a secret? We were about to find out.

VI - Derailed

༈

I knew instantly that something was wrong. As I walked closer to Alex's school, I felt a lump of fear growing in the deepest part of my stomach. Every footstep echoed on the concrete, the vibrations bouncing off my boot and reverberating down the pathway. At the school's entrance, Alex's teacher stood outside with her arms crossed tight against her chest.

My steps slowed.

"Is something wrong?" I asked.

She narrowed her eyes and poked her head down into my personal space, nearly shoving Alex out of the way. "You tell me."

"I don't know what you mean ma'am," I said, slightly quivering.

Alex tried to step out from behind her, but she

slammed her boot down in his way. "Are you going somewhere?"

My heartbeat sped up, and I blinked a little more rapidly than usual. I knew that I had to resist my lifelong training to respect truthfulness and lie. "No."

She pressed her finger into my chest and prodded the t-shirt fabric. "You're not moving?"

My eyes fell on Alex. Did he tell our secret? How else could she know my parents had just given up the apartment? He just stood there, silent, his eyes filled with terror, but I didn't dare give him too much of an angry look.

"It's not true," I said matter-of-factly. "We're not going anywhere."

She pulled back, but her eyes drilled into me. "Alex gave me the impression that your family was preparing to go somewhere."

I nervously laughed and tugged on Alex's arm to drag him towards me. "He's a kid. He talks a lot. They're usually lies."

"Mm hmm," she said.

"We need you in Room 23," another teacher said from behind.

"I'm going to keep my eye on you Alex," she said.

"No need," I said. "Have a good day."

I wrapped my arm around Alex and slowly backed away. My nervous laugh gradually faded, and when the teacher went inside I growled at Alex.

"I didn't say anything," he said. "Honest."

"You better not have or we'll all be in trouble."

We scurried home as quickly as possible. I looked over my shoulder at every passing car, and I was afraid someone would follow us, find us, and lure the truth out of my little brother.

I knew for sure that he would spill the beans about all the interviews we'd been going to, all the background checks, and all the hours spent in the stuffy U.S. government offices as we waited for the official word on when we could leave. With the peace treaty between American President Reagan and the Soviet leader Gorbachev, we finally had the chance to become political refugees.

It was around this time that I was starting to struggle with the idea of leaving. Of course I wanted a better life, but I also knew that it meant saying goodbye to the only home I'd ever known and stepping out into the great unknown.

I walked into the apartment one dreary August day in 1991, just three months before we were scheduled to leave Kiev, and found my mother hunched over on the pullout couch. Her head was buried in her hands and *Swan Lake* was playing on the television. Beads of sweat formed on my brow, as I slowly approached her.

"What's wrong?" I asked.

She didn't lift her head,

"It's Gorbachev," she sobbed through her clasped fingers. "The news conference said he was 'unable to perform his presidential duty for health reasons.' The State Emergency Committee has been appointed."

My heart turned to lead, and I stood rooted to the floor. I had this feeling, this terrible feeling about what was about to happen to us. My parents had already resigned from their jobs. They'd already given up our apartment. With a change in the government, the borders could shut down and we wouldn't be able to leave. We would be homeless, ridiculed, and erased.

Just like the family from the paper.

We later found out that Gorbachev had been under house arrest at his Black Sea residence because eight coup plotters, who included the heads of the army, the KGB, and the police, had tried to overthrow his reign.

Throughout the political unrest, my family remained strong and courageous. Had those eight men, found guilty of treason, not been caught and arrested within the three days Gorbachev was under house arrest, every bad thing we feared could have happened. We would have lost everything. But my parents were steadfast in their decision for us to leave for America no matter the cost. We continued with the interviews and background checks for three long months.

When the time finally came to leave Kiev, it was so surreal that it almost felt like I was watching a movie of someone else's life. I had stuffed my only allotted suitcase so full that the seams were nearly bursting. My entire life's memories were packed into one small rectangular bag. It would be my only physical proof of the USSR chapter of my life.

As for my personal financial resources, I had an entire seventeen cents that a friend had given me for postage to mail a letter back.

I held tight to that fortune. The change felt like gold, clinging to the inside lining of my small pocket. I pressed it as deep as it would go so as not to lose it. I was trusted enough to pay for the postage, so the least I could do was ensure its safe arrival in America.

I knew that I was taking a huge risk. If caught, I could have faced serious repercussions. My parents were only allowed a mere $75 per person. The rest of their belongings that did not fit into two suitcases were sold and the profits, along with the remainder of their savings, had to be given away to friends and family.

The afternoon before we left Kiev, my family made one last trip to put flowers on my grandfather's grave. We were certain that once we gave up our Soviet passports we would never be allowed back into the country, never see his resting place again.

I had brought along his camera. "See Grandpa," I said, "I still have the camera. I'm going to take it with me to America, where I'll take lots of pictures of our new home." I swallowed hard. "Goodbye, Grandpa."

That night I was full of conflicting emotions as I packed my suitcase. How do you choose which parts of your life will stay with you and which ones you will leave behind forever? I had one small bag in which I had to fit everything that was truly important to me.

I carefully wrapped my grandfather's camera in a t-shirt and packed a few other items of clothing around it. I picked up my favorite jeans, thought for a few seconds, then sighed and put them in the pile of things that would stay behind.

Then I picked up the radio that I had built with the help of my father, carefully soldering every connection and screwing every component in place. I smiled at the memory of the first time I turned it on, the first time I heard that brief burst of static hum, and then music playing from my very own creation.

I looked at my suitcase, looked at my radio, and then reluctantly placed it on top of my favorite jeans.

My mother, father, and grandmother were silently going through the same process. There was no room to take along our cherished photo albums, so they were cutting out a few of the most precious photographs. They had already sold or given away their most valuable heirlooms, treasures of our family that had been passed down through generations, treasures that had made it through the Revolution, through World War II, through the Holocaust. Now they were making the last cut.

We were all trimming our entire lives down to one small suitcase each.

I was afraid to tell my parents that I wasn't sure I was completely ready to give up everything. I was excited, but I was also apprehensive. Despite all of Grandpa's speeches about America, I couldn't really know what was waiting on the other side.

And we all knew an even deeper fear, something that none of us wanted to talk about. In preparation for leaving the country we had surrendered our Soviet passports, effectively giving up our USSR citizenship. As far as the government was concerned, we had ceased to exist. This meant that until we could get out of the country, we were vulnerable, completely unprotected.

Since we were no longer citizens, we no longer had any rights. If a gang should chose to rob us, the police would have little interest in pursuing the matter. In fact, during those turbulent days before the final dissolution of the USSR, with the government in chaos, the police were, in a very real sense, the most dangerous gang of all.

We all went to bed, our last night in Ukraine, excited, nervous, and fearful.

In the morning we gathered our belongings and said goodbye to our little apartment, our home, the only home I had ever known. I had my suitcase in my hand, bursting at the seams with my meager wardrobe and my few most prized possessions, and I had my beat-up guitar slung over my shoulder. I walked past the spot on the landing where I had always loved to sit and play that guitar, down the stairs, out of our building, and out of our old life.

We were to take a train to Moscow, where we would board the plane that would fly us to our new home. As we rode through Kiev on our way to the train station, I scanned the skyline of my city, a city of contrasts. We rolled past dull grey concrete buildings and brilliant gold domes; past dull grey adults and laughing children; past dull grey stores with barren shelves and awe-inspiring statues.

I wasn't sure if I should scream from the excitement, smile at the idea of all the opportunities that awaited us, or cry for the loss of all the things I was leaving behind. I looked out as we passed the magnificent Motherland Memorial and wondered if she would ever be able to lift me up and lend me her strength again.

As we neared the train station, I chose to smile. I wanted to believe that things would be better for Alex, for my parents, and for me. I felt the best way I could honor my grandfather was to live out his dream of coming to America.

But twenty-four hours later, on the way to the Moscow airport, our golden dreams weren't just derailed; they were in danger of ending altogether.

VII - Beyond the Horizon

❧

It's amazing what thoughts flash through your mind when you're about to die. You think about what you wish you had done, what you should have done, the promises you never kept, and all the things you dreamed of but would never accomplish. The billion-dollar conglomerate you would never build.

These things all flashed before my eyes as we sat, parked on the side of the winding road on that cold December night in 1991. My heart was pounding, and my throat felt like it had been sandpapered.

I looked to my left where my mother was sitting next to me. I knew she was trying to compose herself, but I could tell from the bead of sweat trailing down the side of her face and how hard she swallowed that she was only pretending to be calm. Alex sat to my right, kicking his feet back and forth nervously. I put my hand on his knee to get him to stop. He shot me a look of annoyance and pressed rebelliously back against my grip. My grandmother sat on the other side of Alex with a face of stone. She laid a hand on Alex's other knee, and that seemed to calm him completely. My father was in the front passenger seat. Though clearly nervous, he composed himself, proving that he was probably the best actor of us all.

Sitting in the driver's seat was the taxi driver, and I prayed that he, of all people, would put on his very best performance as the police officer stuck his head in the window and drilled all of us with questions. Steam billowed from the policeman's nose in the chilly, night air, dancing outside the cab in a condemning cloud. His grey tunic pressed against the window, leaving its mark, a reminder that we would never get away without the officer's permission.

His collar was embellished with gold embroidered leaves, and three gold stars glittered at us from his shoulders. The outline of the officer's machine gun was evident, and when he shifted we caught a glimpse of its cold shine. If we could just stay inside the car, maybe the officer would go away. We all knew that if he asked us to get out, we could be killed.

That moment, frozen in time, sent shivers down my spine.

For years, we had heard horror stories of what happened to people trying to escape the USSR. Like us, they had given up their homes and everything in them. They had sold their last belongings, from dishes, to TVs, to furniture, ridding them of everything that could have tied them to the place they knew as home. And they gave away what was left. There couldn't be a single trace or memory that they'd ever been there once they made the decision. If they were found out before they could leave, bad things happened. They put all their faith into leaving, all their hopes into finding their way to the place where dreams were made. They said their final goodbyes to all their loved ones, just as we had, and then their luck ran out. They were caught.

Maybe someone reported them, maybe it was just bad luck, but they had been pulled aside on the road too, then jailed or shot to death.

I wondered if this would be our fate too, if my last memory would be of the police officer's cold eyes and my parents' terrified faces. It couldn't end that way. I could practically see the airport on the horizon. We were just minutes from freedom, and yet it felt so far away. The thing we had worked toward for years was slipping through our fingers.

Only our prayers could save us now.

I thought about all we had sacrificed, about the close calls, about the lies we had told and the secrets we had hidden, even from our closest friends. Was it all for nothing? Were we to be shot on the side of the road like common, stray dogs?

The officer had our identification papers. He examined them like he was studying for a test or searching pages of a dictionary. We held our breath and watched every movement of his eyes, praying that he would feel generous enough to let us go without asking for anything in return. But in reality, we knew he wanted one of two things: our money or our lives.

Which would it be?

I closed my eyes as tight as I could and prayed. I imagined my grandfather, his dreams for all of us, and how he'd died, in many ways, just inches from the Emerald City.

With a sly smile the officer slipped our identification cards into his back pocket and pulled away from the window. "Get out of the car."

The taxi driver didn't argue with the officer. He didn't even blink. He carefully opened the door and signaled for us to stay where we were. The driver and the police officer exchanged words for a solid five minutes, their voices too low to make out what they were saying. Then, with one quick palm exchange between the two, the officer leaned his head in and offered one more glance. His eyes drilled hard into us.

My mother squeezed my hand tighter.

"You may go," he said. The taxi driver got back inside the car and cleared his throat. We remained silent, knowing full well that the only reason we were able to leave was that the officer didn't want our lives that day. He wanted our money. The taxi driver saved our lives with the few dollars he slipped into the officer's hand. A few minutes, and about a million pounding heartbeats later, we arrived at the airport.

But the end of our journey wasn't even close. Through crowds of sweaty people, we stood in lines for a total of twenty hours with our individual suitcases at our sides. We couldn't sit or lie down. We had to stand. By the time customs searched us, our legs were ready to give out from the wait. They searched every pocket, every crevice, and every possible spot where something could be hidden. They wouldn't allow us to bring anything, aside from our designated luggage.

Through fatigue and boredom, I became mesmerized with the man in front of us. As the customs officers argued with him, their voices strained and grew into a roar. Finally the man pulled a ring off his finger and flung it into the crowd of waiting people. They dove and fought for the wobbly metal band that circled around on the cold floor. We all knew that giving things away to a stranger was better than handing it over to the authorities, but that didn't make it any easier to let go of our most prized possessions.

When it was our turn for inspection, the officer patted my father down first. He was firm and thorough. When it was my turn, his hand traced my pocket and he paused briefly. His eyes jerked up to my father's, and then to mine. He ran his hands over my pocket again, and the seventeen cents jingled just slightly.

He paused.

I wanted to disappear. In the long line of tired people, it seemed as though a spotlight was shining right down on me. I felt the heat from my body rise and threaten to suffocate me. I could see my parents watching helplessly, unable to do anything but stand back as the officer continued patting. After what felt like centuries, the officer's fingers moved away from my pocket, though his stare never left me. He moved on to Alex, then to my mother, and then we were finally given the 'okay' to board the plane.

This was it. It was actually happening.

To this day, I hold a crystal-clear picture in my mind of the way the lights shone on the runway that night. Leaving the USSR, the emotions brimming in all of us, we locked hands and watched Moscow grow smaller as we flew high up into the sky, leaving our old lives behind.

I took a deep, cleansing breath and tried to let my churning stomach settle down. The excitement on my family's faces, beaming through streams of tears, was enough to get me through.

We were headed to Michigan.

The en route plane stopped in Frankfurt, Germany, New York, and Baltimore, and each stop seemed like an endless delay to reaching our final destination, which was Detroit. Between connections, we were prisoners, unable to leave and unable to go where we wanted. We waited hours upon hours between each flight, with weary eyes and aching bones, propping ourselves up against a wall if we were to stand up at all. We didn't sleep for five days straight, and the bags under our eyes grew deeper and deeper.

I was nearly exhausted by all the struggles we were enduring. Would we ever get to our destination? I was ready to live the life my grandfather wanted for us, but this grueling journey was making me think that maybe coming to America was the worst decision we'd ever made.

VIII - Home Free

❦

We finally made it. Once we landed in
Detroit, things didn't feel quite the
way I had thought they would. Landing in America did not turn out to be a magic pill to help me
come to terms with leaving my world behind and
starting anew. In fact, landing in this new country was a shock that I was completely unprepared
for. My head spun from all the noise from the
hundreds of conversations and voices, speaking in
languages I didn't understand.

Everything was completely foreign, and it
didn't matter how confused we were or how much
help we needed. The lights glared down on us,
and the heat forced beads of sweat down our
cheeks. We looked at the signs to try to find out
where we were and where we should go, but all we
understood were the universal figures. Aside from

that, we were like newborn babies experiencing a new world for the first time. Everything was different; the food, the clothing, and even the 33 letters of the alphabet I was used to. In my research, I discovered that English is one of the hardest languages in the world to learn – nearly as difficult as Russian – and this was never more evident than on that day.

We couldn't string together a sentence if we tried. I shoved my hand in my pocket and touched the seventeen cents. It reminded me of home and everything familiar, and it made my heart ache. I was scared and unsure of our decision to travel this new road, but it didn't matter. It's the road we were on.

We would later learn that ninety percent of Ukrainian voters had supported the measure to secure separation from the USSR. We left the Soviet Union on the last day of its formal existence. My life as I had known it, with all the challenges we endured, along with my home country, had literally ceased to exist. We would have truly been homeless if it hadn't been for the political asylum we'd been granted.

By the time we found our relatives, who were there to take us to Ann Arbor, we were exhausted. We left the busy terminal and made our way down the highway where hundreds of cars zoomed by. The weather in Detroit was very similar to Kiev, and I had to keep reminding myself that nothing would ever be the same again. I was tired, hungry, and a little sad. The confusion of the previous five days was almost too much to handle.

When we arrived at our new home, a one-bedroom apartment on the west side of Ann Arbor that had been donated by a local resident, I didn't even unpack my suitcase. This was to be a temporary shelter for us until our government subsidized housing unit was ready.

After our long journey from the USSR, I was in a complete daze, and after a quick look around the apartment, my body gave up altogether. All five of us were completely exhausted and collapsed wherever we could. True to form, my brother and I shared a pullout couch, but I was so tired that I didn't care. I was asleep the instant I closed my eyes.

The next morning, I woke up from a dream about playing hockey with my friends in Kiev, and for a moment I didn't understand where I was. I sat up on my pullout couch and looked around at a living room that was larger than our entire apartment back home. The floors were covered with warm, comfortable carpet, unlike the squeaking hardwood of our old place, and sunlight streamed through a large window. I thought, I must be in some kind of paradise!

I was not aware that this room, that looked so huge to me, was smaller than some Americans' walk-in closets.

Two days after landing in America, I was enrolled in public high school. Since our more permanent home was to be on the other side of town, our school was also on that side of town. This meant that I had to take two different buses just to get to school, and since I didn't know a word of English, my relatives had to sit down and help me draw out basic signs that said things like, "Where is the #3 bus?"

In addition to these challenges, I found that I missed many pieces of my former life. I was deeply conflicted during those first few weeks, and I didn't know if I would ever feel "right" again. On one level, I regretted leaving my old life behind, but I didn't have a choice anymore. It was what it was, so I tried to embrace it.

We remained on the waiting list for the government-subsidized apartment for seven months instead of the three we were told to expect. Alex and I still shared the pullout couch that we folded up whenever relatives came to visit. My grandmother slept on another pullout couch in that magnificent living room, while my parents had the bedroom all to themselves.

A few weeks after our arrival, I found a bicycle

out by the curb with someone's trash and got it working well enough to ride. I didn't care how hard it would be to pedal my bike to school in that cold, ugly winter because it was better than walking or struggling with the bus.

In school itself, the challenges virtually exploded. I couldn't communicate with any of the other kids or make friends. I couldn't understand what the teachers were saying. Learning was more than just difficult; it was nearly impossible. The school felt huge, and I spent my days swimming in a sea of unfamiliar faces and unfamiliar words.

It wasn't long before some of the kids started making fun of me because I didn't speak their language or for the way I dressed. Coming from a longstanding enemy of the U.S., they made me feel like an enemy, an outsider from the very start.

Even though there were many foreigners living in Michigan and the surrounding areas, I felt alone, and I began to miss my old home more than ever. The substantial number of people in Michigan sharing my homeland's bloodline would someday prove to be an overlooked home-buying niche I would divide and conquer. The time leading up to the success I would one day achieve, however, would not be easy.

It would test me in ways I never saw coming.

Photographs

Here I am in 1975 with my mother, Diana and
father, Peter in Ukraine.

This is a photograph of my Grandpa Joseph, my
mom Diana, my Grandma Julia, and Aunt
Svetlana taken in about 1972.

This is me in 1976

Here I am with my Grandma Julia and my
Grandpa Joseph, in 1975.

This is Dr. Joseph Khiterer,
my grandfather and my hero. Not many
photographs exist of my grandfather, since he
owned the camera and was almost always the one
taking the pictures.

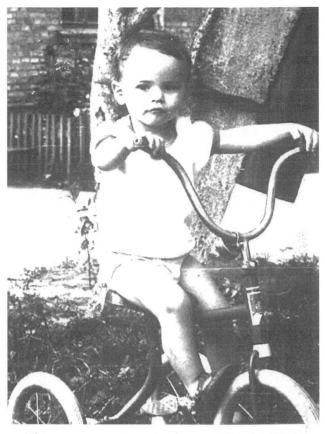

This was my most prized possession in 1978.
My family has very few pictures like this, since
we did not have room in our baggage to take our
photo albums out of the USSR when we escaped.
My parents had to cut from the albums the
pictures they most wanted to keep.

This was an amusement park near Chernobyl.

Kiev, the City of Golden Domes.

The Motherland Memorial in Kiev. This has always been an inspiring sight to me.

Moscow, in many ways a beautiful
and inspiring city.

The Kremlin in Moscow.

I left my first book at the grave
of my grandfather.

My darling daughter Julie.

IX - No Money, No Food

ॐॐ

I was famished. I walked down the giant hill on my way to Farmer Jack, the local grocery store. The ground was steep, rigid, and rocky beneath my shoes. I had to steady myself along the cracks and crevices to get down without toppling over myself. I could hear my stomach rumbling, ordering me to fill it with fuel.

But money was tight. Without job or language assistance for my parents, we were finding it hard to get by. We were on welfare for seven months and couldn't afford even the most basic things such as food.

I lived on a diet of bananas, because they were cheap and nutritious, and I had to eat something to get through the day. There were times my mother would walk three miles, in the dead of winter, just to get the sale ads from the newspaper at the nearby library. She would then make her way to Farmer Jack and use her five-person allotment of $125 per month in food stamps to buy expired food on clearance.

It was all she could do to make sure the five of us had anything at all to eat, and if she couldn't afford it, we managed without. Sometimes, I'd take a bologna sandwich to school for a change of pace, but I mostly ate bananas. The never-ending, gnawing hunger in the pit of my stomach became a part of me and fueled my drive to do more, to be more, so that someday my family could eat without worry.

There were times my family and I would walk to the store together and, because we never saw much food on the bare shelves in the USSR, we would walk through the aisles for hours, just staring at all the items. It was like a museum to us, an inexpensive way to pass the time. We didn't have the money to buy anything, so we would admire the bounty with hungry eyes and then find our way home to the food my mother actually was able to purchase.

During those difficult times we grew very close, bonding over the things we couldn't have and dreaming of the things we might have someday. Despite the financial strain, I enjoyed every moment bonding with my parents through our rumbling bellies.

When I got to Farmer Jack I went up and down every aisle in the store, imagining the different meals I could make with the more expensive items. In the meat department the grumbling in my stomach grew louder and I could almost hear it echoing off the glass of the meat counter as I stared at the beautifully displayed selection of steaks and chops.

I could feel my mouth water, and for a moment I contemplated stuffing a package of steaks down my pants, of taking it home and preparing it for my parents to eat that night at home. I stood and fantasized about the wonderful feeling of defeating the insatiable appetite we'd come to know.

But I was no thief. I shuffled off in search of bananas.

A bit of change, all the cash I had, jingled around in my pockets as I picked up one small bunch of ripe bananas and headed sadly up to the register. I ignored the fact that next to my change was a few dollars in food stamps, because even though we needed them to survive, I was slightly embarrassed to use them.

I paid for the bananas with my change, and then headed back up the hill toward home.

A few weeks later, after a heavy snowfall, I was at the bus stop, making the transfer from one bus to another on my way home from school. Just as I was climbing on the bus, I glanced across the road and saw the most beautiful car in the world; a lipstick red 1986 Pontiac Fiero, with fancy chrome wheels, and a sign on the windshield that said, "For Sale." As the bus pulled away I feasted my eyes on this icon of American automotive perfection.

That night I hardly slept, fantasizing about that red Fiero, what it would be like to drive such a fine sport car. So, the next afternoon after school I walked across the road to the where the car sat, letting my bus go on without me.

It had snowed again overnight, so I carefully brushed off the side window and looked inside. I caught my breath at the sight of the luxurious bucket seats, the gear shifter poking defiantly up out of the center console, and the steering wheel covered with rich black leather.

In the center of the steering wheel a logo was embossed into the leather, a shield that looked as if it might have been copied from the one at the Motherland Memorial in Kiev.

But even as I gazed at this beautiful machine I knew that it was as far out of my reach as the stars. Having grown up in a place where cars were scarce, it should not have mattered to me, but it did. I wanted this car, wanted it badly, to show everyone who had ever bullied me that I wasn't some poor foreigner who was too stupid, too weak, to do anything for himself or to have anything nice.

I turned my back on the Fiero and set off through the snow to walk the three miles home.

Sometimes I would ride my bike two miles to TJ Maxx where a pair of Nike's sat on display. Even though they were half price, I knew I couldn't have them, but sometimes I'd try them on and walk around, pretending that I was somebody who could actually afford such shoes, somebody who didn't have to dress in clothes that were donated.

The only way I could think to make money to buy the things I wanted was to become a bagger at the grocery store. I didn't want to keep walking all the way up that hill with my arms full of bananas and bologna and expired foods. I wanted to drive a red sports car and walk into the store to buy anything I wanted, anything my family needed.

My relatives had given me a universal application that I could memorize, so filling out job applications wasn't terribly difficult. I went to the Kroger store and carefully filled out the form, and within a few days they called me for an interview.

The interview was a disaster. The hiring manager was pleasant enough, but I struggled to understand every question she asked me. And when I tried to answer, I was so nervous that the few words of English I had at my command melted down into pure gibberish. I'm not certain which one of us was more embarrassed and happy to have the interview come to an end.

The car, the shoes, and so many other things would remain just a daydream, because I still didn't know how to get from point A to point B on the ladder of success.

Still, just being in America made that ladder at least possible, and I could begin to see and understand where points A and B were. In America, with enough effort, we could be in the position to buy a car like that someday. In the meantime, we could keep working to buy food and toilet paper. I had dreams, but they were just beginning to really take shape.

I wanted to really learn to speak, read, and write English so I could save myself from the financial distress my parents were fighting so hard to escape. I wanted to remove the stigma all the teachers in the Soviet Union heaped on me, saying that I would never be anything more than a mechanic. Because of the language barrier I faced in America, I couldn't take any of the Advanced Placement courses at school. I wasn't given the chance to succeed.

I found refuge in, oddly enough, an auto shop where I learned the skills necessary to communicate while learning to fix cars. The parents of some of the other kids would say that I was destined to be a mechanic and that, "It's fine if he wants to be a mechanic. That's a good profession too." Who knew that one day I would be providing those same people with reliable financial advice instead of new spark plugs?

I knew that rising above their views of me would be an uphill battle, but I also knew that I was going to make it. I couldn't let people like schoolteachers in Ukraine or bullies get the best of me. I didn't want to stand in a corner, alone, with my bologna sandwich and banana, only to have someone take them from me.

All those other 'cool' kids in their expensive cars and their balanced lunches and cool clothes were enough to motivate me to be more than a mechanic. Even more than the doctor my mother so desperately thought I would be, because that's not who I was but who I am. I was bound and determined to be the best "me" I could be, no matter what obstacles fell in my path.

I had all the tools, and all the things I needed to be somebody. I could fall back on excuses and say that it was too hard; that I wasn't good enough or smart enough. I could have said that everyone picked on me, or that no one thought I could do it. I could have thrown in the towel and apologized to my grandfather for failing, but America was not a place for excuses. It was not going to be a place for failure.

It was going to be a place for opportunities.

I did begin to improve my English, slowly but surely, by taking English as a Second Language classes and watching television. I owe a lot of my conversational skills to the show 'Married… With Children'. My father was fortunate to get a job working nights as a machine operator for $6.75/ hr., and my mother, a former USSR economist, took a whole year to learn English before going to a vocational school and landing a part time job as a medical assistant for $8/hr.

Having gone through the Cold War and the communist regime change, my parents were always thrifty. In fact, after two years of saving, they had enough money for a down payment on a house.

I had a dream that no one could take away from me, a supportive grandmother, and parents who only wanted the best for Alex and me. And I had one thing that no one in the American school could ever take away from me, no matter how much they pushed – courage.

I knew that I could, somehow, stand up to anyone or any thing that stood in my way. I just had to find my path. I had to not only make my grandfather proud, but I had to make myself proud. Hungry, poor, and Russian, or not, I was done with the way things were, done with the old Dan.

X - Bad Kids

꙰

I tried to be a ghost. Everywhere I went, no one really saw me. As my family and I settled in to life in Ann Arbor, it wasn't at all what I had expected America to be. I found myself wandering around town and school by myself a lot, thinking about the ways I could try to fit in, or how I could contribute to my family's finances.

My only friend in those days was my third cousin, Gene. He'd come to America with my uncle in 1980, but Gene wasn't like me. He was only six when his parents fled for the US before the 1980 Olympic Games, before the borders were sealed. His Russian was so terrible that he couldn't even understand when his parents said curse words. I was the one who told him what his own parents were saying in Russian. To my dismay, my Russian accent was still thick despite my every effort to learn English. This is probably why I was tortured for so long.

Walking down the halls at school, I'd hang my head low and keep my eyes on the floor. I couldn't make eye contact, or they would find something to mock. I couldn't move the wrong way or they would imitate me. If I heard kids laughing, I didn't dare look up.

Seven months after we arrived in Ann Arbor, we moved to our government-subsidized apartment. We now had two bedrooms, so Alex and I had our own room to share. My grandmother had a government-subsidized apartment of her own, so nobody had to sleep in the living room.

My parents were working, but we still had barely enough money for the basic necessities. Among other things, we were still living on bananas and bologna. One evening after school I had walked to the nearby Kroger to pick up a bunch of bananas for our evening meal.

Standing in line, I heard footsteps behind me, and an eerie feeling made my hair stand on end.

I turned to see a big yellow-haired boy with cruel eyes staring down at me. I recognized Doug from school, but I was too embarrassed to say anything. I felt that he somehow knew that this small bunch of bananas was all my family would have to eat. I turned away from him and back to the cashier.

When the cashier asked for the money, I spilled my change all over the floor and then nervously scraped up each and every penny. After I completed my transaction, I looked around for Doug, but he was gone.

"Your receipt," the cashier said, but I was already on my way out the door. I couldn't run fast enough. I didn't really know Doug, but he always seemed to turn up wherever I was. It was as if he had it in for me, like some of the other kids at school. Being different wasn't just a challenge; it was a daily struggle nearly everywhere I went. The only response I had was to hold my head up high and try to keep a smile on my face, no matter how tough some days were.

Just as I walked through the automatic door and into the parking lot, Doug stepped out from behind a van and ripped the bananas from my hand.

"Thanks, asshole, I can use a little snack," he said as he strolled away with my family's dinner.

I stood there for a few minutes with my head pounding. Then empty handed and hungry, I headed for home.

After the banana incident, Doug waited for me every morning at my locker. He would watch as I nervously twisted and turned the little knob back and forth to no avail, laughing and mocking as I wasted valuable learning time. I tried to ignore him, but that only seemed to fuel the fire.

One afternoon Doug followed close behind me after school. I'd been kept over in my last class, and I was afraid of missing the bus so I was walking at a brisk pace. Doug didn't say a word as his shoes nipped at the backs of my heels, so I walked faster. My books started to slip from my hands.

I meant to head toward the bus entrance, but I was so disoriented that I couldn't see or think about where I was going. I turned a few corners and sped down a couple of ramps in the big, still unfamiliar building, ending up in an empty storage room. There was no janitor. There was no one, only the school's thundering, steaming furnace.

This time Doug didn't want bananas; he was out for blood. I was terrified by the cold lack of emotion in his eyes. It was as if he couldn't hear or see me once his mind was set on going after me. I didn't know what I had done to create this monster in front of me, but I wished I hadn't.

I backed into a corner, dropping all of my books but one, and pressed my spine against the wall. Doug stood a few feet away and looked me over with an evil smirk.

"Why don't you go back to where you came from, shithead?" he asked, walking towards me.

I couldn't speak. My lips quivered. The closer he came, the more I shook. I was used to being picked on, but this was different. This was a hatred worse than anything else I had experienced in America.

Doug stopped about an inch from me. His face loomed over mine.

"Answer me!" he demanded.

"I-I-I-" I stammered.

"Shut up. Just give me your money!"

I emptied my pockets to reveal only holes and a crumpled food stamp. Even if I could have spoken, I wouldn't have. I didn't want to antagonize him even further with the way I talked. He shoved his hands into my chest and pushed me hard into the wall. My body bounced off, and I waved my arms to catch myself from falling. As I wobbled around, I fell into him. He cocked a fist back and sucker-punched me deep into my gut. He hit me so hard that I doubled over and felt my lunch rise up in my throat. I squeezed the book between my hands so tight that I should have left fingerprints.

Doug laughed, grabbed the food stamp and shoved it into his pocket. "Broke-ass little commie. You're pathetic."

As he turned to walk away, so confident and cocky, I'm not sure what got into me. I felt my arms lift themselves from my sides, raising the book above my head, and I felt a white-hot fury take control of me. In that moment, I thought about all the other kids who had made me feel less than human during my first few months in this land of dreams.

I ran towards Doug and tackled him from behind, smacking the back of his head with the book. He rolled over, kicking and swinging with his eyes shut tight. In the middle of it all, a fire alarm sounded which seemed to startle Doug. It also distracted me long enough to pause, so that Doug managed to escape from my grip. But instead of coming after me, he did something I never expected – he ran away.

As he retreated from the dark room he bellowed back at me, "You'll be sorry!" I caught my breath and composed myself, bending over to pick up my pile of books with trembling hands. I didn't feel good about what had happened, but on some level I felt a little better knowing that I could defend myself if I was pushed too far.

Doug didn't bother me from that point on, and about a month later his body was discovered with a gunshot wound to the head. Rumors spread that he had been playing Russian roulette with another kid and lost. I was surprised to find that I actually felt a sort of sadness for him. It seemed shameful for anyone to totally waste a life. I certainly was not going to miss him, though.

When things settled down at school, I again found myself wandering the halls. One day I ended up by the gym where a group of kids sat, undeniably "cool" with their cigarettes and their "I don't care" attitudes. I wanted to know them. I meandered towards them and casually leaned up against the wall, trying to blend in.

"So do you think Doug did it?" one of them asked another.

"What? The robbery at Kroger?" the girl replied. "I know his dad lost his job and they didn't have money for food or anything. We haven't been friends in a long time, but I totally think he did it. He kind of lost it."

"What do you think?" the girl, whose name I knew was Irene, asked me.

I tried to compose my thoughts so I didn't sound like an idiot, because my English was still nearly non-existent. "I didn't know him."

"Oh," she replied.

Irene was the kind of pretty that could have gotten me into trouble. She was in a couple of my classes, and it seemed like she was always involved with any classroom drama. I watched transfixed as her ruby lips pursed to draw a puff from her cigarette. I pretended not to be affected, or to cough, when she blew her smoke in my direction. She looked at me with eyes that could melt copper, and I thought my heart was going to stop. I tried not to tremble as I stared straight ahead at the paint on the wall.

I must have played the ghost well enough to suit them that day, because they didn't tell me to get lost. They just kept talking and smoking and ignored me, so I decided that this must mean that I was "in."

I thought that I had found a place among these kids who didn't care what anyone thought, and the idea of that was exhilarating. I thought that with Doug out of my life and some new friends to hang out with, everyone else would ease up, and the worst times would be behind me.

XI - Alone

꙳

It was the first hard snowfall of the winter. My new "friends" bantered back and forth at the backdoor of the gym after lunch, ignoring me as I stood silently around the corner and listened. They were crowded around one another for warmth, their hands jammed into their pockets and cigarettes hanging from their lips.

"So, this weekend then?" said Craig, the guy with slicked-back dark hair. He blew a stream of smoke from the corner of his mouth.

I leaned my head around the corner a bit. Every day I'd been following them out for their after-lunch smoke so that I could "accidentally" bump into them. I was still looking for the nerve to walk right up to them and become part of the conversation.

"I don't know," Irene said. " It sounds kind of lame."

I leaned out a little more, maybe too much, and my backpack scraped against the tiles.

"Hey," said Craig. "You."

I froze.

"It's Dan, right?"

I shuffled around the corner. I could feel Irene's eyes on me as I nodded.

"Come hang," he said.

I tried to look cool, even in the donated shirt that had a slight rip on the chest. I held my books against my chest to hide the tear, a pose that was probably more awkward and uncomfortable than anything else, but they acted like they didn't notice.

"So are we going sledding this weekend or what?" asked Craig. He was the obvious leader of the pack, shrewd and a bit arrogant. Even when I could make out what he was saying, I found it difficult to know if he was being sarcastic.

Even though he was clearly addressing his question to everyone but me, I couldn't stop myself from saying, "I'd love to go sledding!" As soon as the words left my lips, I could feel my knees begin to chatter. They couldn't possibly want to go sledding with me. Could they?

He turned, inhaled slowly, and blew a smoke ring almost directly at me. I watched, fascinated, as it grew larger and closer, and then dissolved in the cold air. "You think you can hang with us?"

I didn't understand the question. I thought I already was "hanging" with them. The intensity in his eyes grew, and he stepped closer to me. Craig had never said more than two words directly to me, and here I was, crashing their plans. I hoped that they liked me, and it didn't matter to me that they might not be the best crew to cling to. They weren't making fun of me at that moment, and that was good enough. I was tired of being lonely, and I just wanted someone other than my family to talk to.

"Yeah, I can hang with you," I said, unsure of myself, of them, of anything. My words seemed to hang in the air, visible, painted with the unmistakable brush of my Russian accent. I tried to slow my pulse but the more I tried, the more it raced. Irene giggled and her eyes, the color of ice, latched on to mine. I felt a strange twinge, as if a hook was digging into my heart. I smiled back.

"Cool," he said, wrapping his arm around Irene. I thought I saw her try to shrug him away. "What's your number? I'll give you a call."

"I don't have a phone," I said, embarrassed.

"No phone? That is rough!" said one of the

other boys, with a laugh that reminded me of the braying of a donkey.

"I didn't have a phone for like a month when we moved," Irene interrupted. "It's not that bad." She smiled at me again.

I smiled back again.

"So how are we supposed to get hold of you?" the other boy asked. "Should we send you a telegram? How about a carrier pigeon?" They all laughed. Irene looked the other way and concentrated her attention on her cigarette.

"I'll give you my cousin Gene's number. You can call him," I said. My face felt hot, red, and flushed.

"Yeah okay, write it down," Craig demanded.

I pulled a pencil from my bag and scribbled Gene's number and my address, as quickly as I could. I needed to get their eyes off me.

He furrowed his brow as he read the address. "That's the, ah, project clear up on the north side of town."

We all lingered in the awkward silence that lasted until the bell rang, startling me.

"So we'll plan on picking you up tonight around seven o'clock," Irene said, stepping on her cigarette butt.

"Yeah, sounds good," I said, slinging my backpack over my shoulder. I tried not to seem too eager but the excitement growing inside me was nearly bursting through my skin.

"If something changes, I'll call," said Craig as he threw his arm around Irene and guided her down the hall. Everyone went their separate ways while I stood in the stale smoke smell and thought about what had happened.

I had friends.

I couldn't wait to get home and for them to pick me up later that night. I didn't have expensive snow gear, or any snow gear at all, but that didn't matter. I wasn't even hungry for my usual banana and bologna. I just wanted to go. I alerted my cousin Gene of the possible phone call.

"Why would you want to hang with those losers?" he asked.

I ignored the question and piled on as many warm clothes as possible. Gene told me that my parents had been asking about the kind of kids I was hanging out with, but he covered for me. I hadn't even realized that my new friends were the kind of kids I would need a cover story for. It felt so exciting.

When evening came around, I stood outside our apartment wearing my makeshift sledding gear and waited. It was a bitter kind of winter cold that chewed away at my flesh, but to me it was worth it. I caught my breath with each headlight that moved towards me and then sighed with disappointment as it passed on by. I blew hot air into my palms and rubbed them together to create the friction to keep me warm. My ears were numb from the brisk Michigan wind.

Seven o'clock came, and seven o'clock went.

They're running late I told myself. The minutes turned to hours. By the time I knew it, it was nearly the middle of the night and no one had shown up to get me. I asked Gene if they had called, and he just shook his head.

The friends I thought I'd made had ditched me, left me standing alone in the angry winter night. No matter how hard I tried, I couldn't escape the loneliness.

The following Monday at school, I found them once again smoking by the gym.

"Where were you guys Friday?" I asked.

Craig looked back at me coolly. "Oh, sorry," he said, barely acknowledging me. "I didn't know that was for sure." The others said nothing. Irene offered one quick glance and then turned away too. My heart sank and I tried to play it cool, but even as I was struggling to think of the right thing to say, the four of them scattered.

"Gotta go," said Craig. "Later."

I stood there feeling like I was some sort of

disease they couldn't wait to get away from. I grabbed my backpack from the floor and wandered around the building until the bell rang. This same thing happened every day for the next week. I didn't know what I had done wrong, but something inside me told me that enough was enough. I needed something bigger and better.

And it was about to come to me in the form of a clown named Ronald.

XII - Cinderella Story

৯৽৽ৡ

Every day was a struggle. Even at sixteen I didn't have the luxury of dwelling too long on losing any "friends." To keep me occupied, and to help the family out, I applied for every job I could find. I became fluent in the language of job applications. With every new place I'd apply for work, I'd walk out the door of our apartment in the projects daydreaming about what it would feel like to be able to live in a better place, to afford retail clothes, and to take care of my family. I thought about how great it would be to buy more than bananas, and to pay with money instead of the food stamps my mother kept crunched in her palm until the very last minute when it was time to pay. I wanted to save her, and myself, from the humiliation she experienced at each trip to the grocery store.

In the meantime, my father and I would deliver newspapers or provide landscaping services for local residents, a situation that didn't always go so well. There was one time when we discovered that since we didn't understand property lines, we had not only landscaped the yard of the professor who had hired us, but we had serviced the neighbor's yard as well. Everything involved with coming to America was a learning process.

One day after school, after we'd finally gotten a phone installed in our apartment, there was a note that someone had called. I looked over the scribbles and discovered that the call was from the manager of the local McDonald's, a restaurant I had never been to until the day I filled out the job application. I walked over to the phone and nervously dialed, swallowing so often that, as I listened to the phone ringing at the other end, a dry cough formed in the back of my throat. I feared that my accent and lack of English would prove to be too big a barrier, but when the man answered he asked me to come in for an interview.

"I'm so proud of you!" my mother said, hugging me tight.

"I didn't even get the job yet," I told her.

"It doesn't matter. I'm still proud of the man you're becoming."

"What's McDonald's?" Alex asked. "What will you do?"

"Calm down, sweet boy," mother said, patting Alex's head. "He'll tell us when he knows more."

I slouched over to the table and sank into my chair. I felt like the weight of everyone's expectations was pressing hard on my shoulders, and I couldn't afford to fail. I had to be "five times better than everyone else," just as my parents always taught me. Anything less meant that I wasn't paying them back for all they had sacrificed. If this interview was my only chance, I had to be sure that I made a lasting impression.

The next day I put on my best clothes and rode my bike through the falling rain to McDonald's. The droplets stung my cheeks, but I didn't care. I laid my bike up against a metal pole and opened the big, daunting doors. Inside, people hustled and bustled behind a giant counter. The smell of French fries and hamburgers enveloped me. With the lingering hunger deep inside me, it all smelled so good.

"Daniel?" the hiring manager said, waving me towards an empty booth. I followed close behind him and sat down. He ran through a general explanation of the job and then began asking me questions. I didn't understand much that was said through what seemed like an agonizingly long interview, but I nodded my head and tried to appear as if I was grasping every word.

"If we're interested, we'll call you," he said as I left. I just nodded and inhaled one last breath of the delicious aroma that I knew I wouldn't get to actually taste.

As I pedaled my bike along the long journey home through the unforgiving downpour, the details of the job were running through my mind. Could I do it? I pedaled and I pedaled. I was looking at the road, but I don't remember seeing it. The gloom in the sky, the rain, and even the cold seemed to retreat as I surrendered to my personal fantasy of working in that wonderful place.

Mid-daydream, I pedaled right through a stop sign just as a car was coming through. My head jerked. The car slammed on its brakes, screeching and sliding into a large puddle. Crashing back to reality, I paused for a moment, looked at the car, at the stop sign, and tried to catch my breath. I could hear the wind pick up along with the thunder. The man driving the car rolled his window down and shouted,

"Watch where you're going kid!" and pumped his fist in the air.

I couldn't speak. I put my feet back to the pedals and headed home as fast as I could. When I got there, I hunkered down in front of the phone and waited.

It was only a few hours before the phone rang. "You have the job if you want it," the manager said. I felt myself grinning so hard that my mouth nearly ripped. My parents and Alex crowded around, waiting for the final news.

"I got it," I said quietly. Everyone jumped and screamed with excitement, pride beaming from their faces. This was it. This was my moment, and I savored it as long as I could, because I knew it was my chance to make a real difference in my family. To most Americans, this type of job might seem trivial, even a short-term annoyance. For me it was a lifeline, an opportunity to get a fresh start.

On my first day at work I was nervous. My hands had been shaking all morning. They gave me a uniform, which I quickly put on, and a mop. But there was one problem: I didn't know what a mop was. The lady who was training me smiled, grabbed my hand, and physically wrapped my fingers around the mop's handle. She didn't seem to mind going the extra mile, but there were others who were not so patient with me.

"Take out the trash," one girl said, throwing a bag at me.

"Scrub the toilets when you're finished," another added.

"The dishes after that," a man joined in.

My typical day under the Golden Arches started at five in the morning, and I worked three hours until eight. Then I would go to school hungry, because there was no time and I didn't want to spend money for breakfast. Then I'd go back to work after school until bedtime. Those days were long and often hard, but I was doing everything possible to help my family and to make something of myself.

Around this time, I started talking with two other Russian students in my school, whose families had come to America a few years earlier. We bonded over our similar experiences and hardships, and agreed that American-born students often seem to take it for granted that we live in this limitless land of possibility. Anything could happen in America. In history class, the teacher sometimes talked about immigrants who overcame obstacles by coming to America, and the first people I thought of were my parents. They embodied everything those famous names did and more.

I was inspired, along with my two Russian friends, to take a road trip to New York with my third paycheck. We traveled to Ellis Island, a place that had been the gateway to a new life for millions of people, and wandered through the museum. We studied hundreds of old photos of people before us who had traveled here by boat to start anew.

I wondered what it must have been like to step foot onto American soil and see the Statue of Liberty as opposed to an airport terminal. It brought tears to my eyes to read about the obstacles those people had to overcome to be there.

When I got home from New York I painted the Golden Arches on the wall over my bed, as a reminder of the promise of my adopted country.

Not everyone had as much regard as I did for those Golden Arches. One day at work, while I was scrubbing each and every tile with the mop that I had come to know so well, the pack of kids from school came through the double doors. I kind of panicked over what Irene might think about my mop and pail, so I ran behind the divider wall and stood as still as a statue, with the mop against my chest. I waited while they ordered and hoped they wouldn't see me. My eyes were shut tight, and I actually held my breath.

"Dan," a voice said. I squeezed my eyes tighter.

"Dan. Hello?" It was Roger, the manager on duty, tapping my shoulder. "Back to work."

I slowly opened my eyes to see the group of boys and Irene standing directly behind him, all of them laughing.

"Sorry," I mumbled, swishing the mop back and forth with my head down.

"Hey, man" one of the boys said. "That's a real cool uniform."

They walked by me to sit down, whispering and giggling along the way. Irene didn't say anything, but as she passed, her eyes reeled me in as they always seemed to do. She flashed what I thought must be a sympathetic smile and made her way to the booth. I turned away and mopped as fast as I could.

While they ate, I was aware of their eyes following me. The moment felt like a scene in a play, frozen in time with me in the center of the stage and a huge spotlight shining down on me. I tried to look as cool as possible with my hairnet, but all I got back from them were more laughs. My co-workers caught on, but instead of helping me out, they joined in.

"You missed a spot," said the cashier, as he opened a packet of ketchup and dribbled it across the floor. He pressed his boot into the red blob and smeared it. As he walked away, ketchup covered footprints followed him back behind the counter. The kids at the table laughed so hard that they nearly fell out of their seats. Irene wasn't laughing, but she wasn't defending me either.

I wanted to crawl in a hole and die.

I swirled the mop in the water and cleaned up the mess, but the stain in my heart couldn't be so easily rinsed away.

XIII - Sleep Doesn't Work Here

❧❧

In 1992, jobs were hard to come by, so I was grateful for even the uniform and the hairnet. When I received my first check, it was like winning the lottery. My parents hung the stub high up on the wall where it still sits to this day.

Starting with that check, I saved $5 each pay-day for a particular pair of white Nike's with the green swoosh that I tried on every day in the shoe store, even though I knew I couldn't afford them. It wasn't until months later, when I was headed home after a long shift, that I had enough cash to purchase the sneakers. It took so long to save the money that by the time I could pay for them, they had been reduced to the clearance rack, but I didn't care. I worked hard for them, I earned them, and I finally had them.

Even with my half-off employee discount, I didn't want to spend precious money on the fifty-two cent hamburgers that everyone else enjoyed on breaks. I had to save every penny, no matter how hungry I was. Day after day I watched other workers carry home bags of food and shakes to their families. I could only imagine how it must have felt to eat the food I smelled all day. It wasn't until three months and a few paychecks later that I decided to splurge and try one of our hamburgers.

After I worked my way up from scrubbing floors to taking orders, I found that I mostly enjoyed working the morning shifts. Many of the people were friendly and happy on their way to start their days, and they took their time enjoying their breakfast. Some of them even seemed to like my Russian accent, and they joked with me good-naturedly as I rang up their orders.

I had quite a few regular morning customers. I didn't know their names, but I knew their breakfasts, and that's how I would think of them. Good morning, Mr. McMuffin, hash Browns, and coffee! My regulars were pleased when I saw them coming and had their choices rung up for them before they even got to the register. Of course, I could easily have changed the order if they changed their minds, but they never did.

During those morning shifts at McDonald's I learned what is, in many ways, the most valuable thing I ever learned as a salesman: if you show a customer you sincerely care about them enough to remember that they like room in their coffee for cream, they will love doing business with you, and they will go out of their way to do so.

None of this came easy though. In school, after working my morning shift at McDonald's, I was painfully aware that I smelled like a quarter pounder with cheese. After school I would head straight back to the restaurant to work another shift, staying on my feet until they ached with fatigue. I was always tired, but I was also proud that I was able to take care of my family and to make something of myself, to honor the wishes of my grandfather.

As my junior year of high school came to a close, the hours of work started adding up, and I found myself running on empty for days at a time. Sometimes, after a long shift of cleaning floors, washing dishes, and hauling trash, my muscles and bones were ready to give up, and my brain would be turned to mush.

"Dan," the shift manager said one day, waving me over. It was the end of my second shift that day and my feet had begun to tingle. I walked over, ready to clock out, go home, and eat. I felt like I could barely stand and waves of fatigue passed through me.

"Can you work an extra shift?" he asked. "We need another set of hands."

I rubbed my eyes. "Sure, when?"

"Right now."

My first thought was to scream. The second was to run. The third, which I paid attention to, prompted me to shut up and do it, because my family needed the money.

"No problem."

I trudged back behind the counter and wiped everything down. I watched as the other employees clocked out happily and made their way home or to wherever they were going. I wished it could be me, because I had a big test the next morning at school, but it didn't matter. If they were paying me, I was there. But after serving orders, washing three loads of dishes, mopping the floor twice, cleaning all four toilets and taking out five bags of trash, I hit my limit.

I excused myself to the bathroom, locked the door, and slid to the floor, my back against the wall. I caught my head in my hands, and felt fatigue draining through my body. Then, like a dam bursting open, I began to cry into my hands. I tried to stay quiet, so no one could hear, but the tears fell faster than I could wipe them away. I closed my eyes and told myself it would all be okay.

I thought about Kiev. I heard the angry voices of the mob in the streets outside our apartment. I thought about Chernobyl. I thought about Moscow. I saw visions of my hardworking parents doing everything in their power to take care of Alex and me. I saw teachers yelling at me for being stupid, for being nothing.

Somewhere in all those images I found a new strength, so I stood up, washed my face, and dusted myself off. I was Daniel Milstein, and I was not going to give up. I went back to work stronger than before. I declared war on that job. I did everything they asked of me, no complaints, no more tears.

When I was finally able to clock out, I rode my bike the many miles home, where everyone was fast asleep.

I crept to the fridge and pulled out the bologna to make a sandwich. I sat down with a slice of meat in one hand and a slice of bread in the other and just for a moment closed my eyes. When I woke up, the sun was shining on the kitchen table. I was still in my uniform, still hungry, and still clutching my unmade sandwich.

Looking up at the clock, I realized that Daniel Milstein was going to be having that bologna sandwich for breakfast as he pedaled back to McDonald's for his morning shift.

After six months, I decided that it was time for me to move up in the company. I wanted to train to be more and to earn more. I was working harder than anyone around me, so I thought it was only right. One cold November day I found Roger in the back office. He was crunching numbers as usual, and working his way through a box of fries. I had waited until after my shift so I would not leave any of my duties undone. I didn't know quite what to expect, but I felt hopeful. Roger was, after all, the one who gave me my shot in the first place.

"Sir," I said, approaching the doorway.

"Come in, Dan," he said.

"Sir, I was wondering when I might be ready for a promotion."

He looked at me over his thick-framed glasses and stopped chewing. "A what? Promotion? You're not ready for that."

"But, sir, I've been working really hard and taking extra shifts, and I'd like to do more."

He went back to scribbling in the chart, grabbed another fry from the box and said, "No, kid. You're not ready."

"But, sir," I said.

"Get back to work."

"I'm off now."

He looked up once more and smiled. "I need you to come back tonight and pick up an extra shift. Can you do that?"

I looked at the green and white paper on his desk with the Golden Arches logo in the upper right hand corner. I pinched the fabric in my empty pockets and scuffled my feet to cover up the sound of my grumbling stomach. It was eight in the morning and time for school.

"I'll be here."

XIV - Drive-Thru Blues

৵৽

N obody wanted to do it. Michigan isn't just cold in December; it's arctic. When Roger asked for a volunteer to work the drive-thru, everyone else scattered as I stood there, holding my mop and translating what he had just said.

"Thanks!" He patted my back. "Way to be a team player." He tossed the drive-thru headset to me and walked away.

I stood there and thought about those Golden Arches on my bedroom wall and smiled. No matter what, I was proud to work for a company like McDonald's, to be part of the team, even when it meant freezing at the drive-thru window. Besides, I've been to Siberia. Who knew better than me what winter was all about?

I set the mop inside the bucket and let it drop against the wall, hooked the headset over my ear and walked to the drive-thru, where the frigid wind sliced through the cracks around the window. My jacket was hanging in the back room but I didn't want to leave my station to get it, so I stood in the icy breeze and started taking orders.

Between customers I blew hot air into the palms of my hands and did a sort of shuffling dance to keep warm. It took a few cars for me to get the hang of the order process, but I eventually got into the rhythm of working the window. The other employees stayed near the front and laughed at the Russian guy dancing in the drive-thru. No one offered to switch with me, or take turns, or to help me out at all. I eventually stopped caring. As cold as it was, and as much as I still struggled with my accent, I was starting to do a pretty good job.

And then she came through.

"Welcome to McDonald's," I said. "How may I help you?"

Silence...

"Welcome to McDonald's," I repeated. "Order whenever you're ready."

A giggle blasted through my ear bud. "Sorry," she said. "I'll take a number one with a diet Coke and a number four with an iced tea."

I knew that voice. I groaned to myself as I punched the numbers into the register and gave her the total. "Pull around when you're ready."

My heart sped up as the car slowed down, and a head poked out from the driver's side. Irene.

I pushed the lever to open my window. "Hi," I croaked.

"Hey, Dan," she said. "How's it going?"

"Not too great if he's working here," her friend said from the passenger seat.

I kept my eyes glued to Irene and pretended not to hear her friend. Irene's hair was in big, bouncy curls and she smiled at me with those fire engine red lips. She elbowed her friend in the ribs and asked, "How much is it again?"

I leaned on one hand to keep my balance and held my gaze too long, wondering what it would be like to really know her, to ride in her car. Maybe some wonderful day I might even get to go on a date with her.

"Hello?" she said, waving her hand around in the air.

"Come on, dude!" her friend yelled. "We're hungry!"

I shook myself out of my daydream and looked back at the register to discover that I had unintentionally been leaning on the keypad, messing up the total. I started pressing buttons, lots of buttons, but nothing made it better. I flashed a mortified smile as the two girls began to laugh.

"So, how much?" she repeated. She waved a ten at me.

"It's freezing!" her friend shouted.

I pounded on the register, but it just kept beeping at me. Pretty soon, just about everyone in McDonald's was watching. Another car had pulled up to order. The man was growing impatient, yelling into the speaker for me to take his order.

"Just one moment, sir," I said, hitting the register harder.

Roger raced over to see what the commotion was about. "Dan, what's the problem?"

"I, uh, the register is locked," I stammered.

Roger assessed the situation, then leaned out the window and handed Irene their food. "I'm sorry about your wait. This is on Dan. Have a nice night."

"Later, Dan," Irene said. "Thanks for dinner!"

"Yeah, thanks, DAN!" her friend giggled and waved her iced tea at me. Irene rolled up her window and drove away.

"Sir, I can't pay for their food," I told Roger.

"I'll take it out of your check."

"But, sir, my family needs that money."

"Listen Dan, I have a business to run. I'll let it go this time. But in the future, don't break my register and don't make my customers wait in the cold for their hot food." He pushed a key into the register's keyhole and twisted. The drawer popped open and the beeping stopped. "Now get back to work."

I stood for a moment, watching Roger walk away and replaying the last few minutes in my mind. Well, there was my big date – with Roger's help, I'd taken Irene out to dinner.

The window was still wide open, but considering the head of nervous steam I'd built up, the breeze felt nice. I let the chill hit my cheeks, let it sting a little as I took and filled the order for the impatient young man at the speaker. I was almost back to normal by the time I handed him his change and his food.

He didn't say a word as he tossed his change into his ash tray, tore the end off the wrapper of his straw, and blew a perfect straw wrapper rocket that hit me in the forehead, right between the eyes.

As he drove away from my window, my co-workers howled with laughter, falling over counters and gasping for air. Some of the customers even joined in.

I chuckled to myself and tossed the straw wrapper into the trash. As I took the next order I thought about a day when I might be the boss, running the place. I wanted to decide who would mop the bathroom. I wanted to have the key to the register. I wanted to make sure that all the employees took turns at the drive-thru.

Then I realized that what I really wanted to be was the man who was in a position to give a passionate immigrant a chance. I wanted to give some kid a job that would inspire him to paint the Golden Arches on his wall.

XV - One Chance is All it Takes

☙❧

They said it couldn't be done. Nearly a whole year had come and gone, and each day at McDonald's began to feel like a repeat of the day before. I cleaned so many toilets, scrubbed so many dishes, wiped so many counters, mopped so many tiles, and hauled so many bags of trash that it all felt like a greasy blur. I was mostly running the drive-thru, even after the weather warmed up, because I was actually good at it. But even though I enjoyed the work, there were still those days when someone would drive through just to laugh at the Russian guy.

So in 1993 when McDonald's announced the details of the new All American competition, I jumped at the chance. The deal was that whoever won the series of competitions would automatically be sent into the management training program. I saw this as an amazing opportunity.

"You're not going to enter that, are you?" Roger said as I looked over the application. "Then who would run my drive-thru?"

I smiled up at him for just a moment then continued re-reading the application and the list of prizes on the back. I could see dollar signs, advancement, and accolades from the higher-ups. Even though I had grown into my job at McDonald's, I wanted the chance to make something more of myself, not just be the drive-thru guy. More than that, I wanted respect.

"I think I can win it," I said to Roger.

"Good luck with that," he chuckled as he walked away.

"You're not going to win," one of the cashiers said. She'd only been there a month and already treated me like the others did.

"Why not," I asked.

"First of all," she said, "you have to speak English."

"I do."

"Not well."

I bit my tongue because I knew she was right. I still couldn't speak the native language very well, but I wasn't stupid. I understood everything just fine, and I knew, no matter what they said, that I could win.

On the following shift I brought a small pad of paper and pen to study for the competition. I noted the cooking times and temperatures, French fry sizes, holding times, oil content, any information I could get my hands on without anyone noticing. While working the drive-thru, I would stuff the notebook in my pocket, and when I worked the counter I'd pull it out and scribble as much as I could. When I'd get home my eyes would be sore, burning from squinting at that notebook. I tried hard to make each word stick in my memory, and I even had my parents quiz me. They learned a lot about special sauce and walk-in refrigerators.

Between my early morning shift, school, my evening shift, and studying, I had almost forgotten what it felt like to be a human. I was running on empty. And through it all, it seemed that there was always someone there to mock and belittle my every attempt to learn.

That is why I studied harder.

I turned in my application and began the first supervised test of many in an ordeal that would last more than ninety days. Stores all across the country were competing, and there were a lot of applicants, but I wasn't just up against everyone else. I was up against myself. I needed to prove that I could do it.

I was nervous, sweating through my uniform. After writing down the last answer, the correct temperature for the French fries, and turning in my test, my results were recorded and sent on to the executives in charge of the competition. I had no way of knowing if I'd done well or not, and it was that way for every other test in the competition.

Ninety days later, after the final scores were tallied, my parents and brother sat on a bench in the store, waiting to hear if I'd made the cut or not. I tried to get them to go home, but I knew they wouldn't budge until they knew the results. When the executives made their way in, one shake of the hand and I knew I'd won. For the first time in my life, I was standing out for doing something well, not because of my accent or being poor or eating so many bananas. I was being recognized because I had excelled at everything they threw at me. I had proved to everyone who had expected me to fail that they were wrong, and I had won. This is a fantastic career move, I thought. I was already planning the ways I could help my family.

"Great job, Daniel," the district manager said. He introduced me to his colleagues, the ones in charge of the whole competition. They shook my hand and gave me a friendly pat on the back.

"Welcome to the management training program son," one of the men said. He handed me a certificate and a stack of papers about what I was getting into. It didn't matter what the fine print said. At the age of eighteen I was about to become the shift manager, supervising about thirty employees. To this day, I see that moment as a testament to how important it is to be proud of the work you do, no matter if it's scrubbing toilets or making multi-million dollar sales. I gave my all to everything I did, and it was beginning to pay off.

My parents ran over to congratulate me.

"I'm so proud of you!" my mother said.

"Well done," my father said.

"Um, awesome job," a voice said from behind me. "Way to climb up the fast food ladder."

I turned around to see the leader of the pack, laughing with the others. Irene waved slightly as if they embarrassed her.

"Up next, you'll be the CEO of the school cafeteria. Big thumbs up dude. You see? In America, dreams do come true."

I chuckled at him as he walked away, slurping through his straw. I clutched my certificate of recognition and thought about how things would change for me with this new opportunity. It was okay that it didn't mean the same thing to other people as it meant to me. I wanted it, and I needed it. My family needed it. There was no security blanket for me to go home to. I was creating my own security blanket.

The next day at school, I was so proud of myself that I felt bigger, taller almost. I probably smiled most of the day, and I didn't care that I still smelled of the previous night's Big Macs. Graduation was near, and so was my future. When I passed the pack of kids in the hallway, their insults didn't even get to me.

Well, not as much.

I was starting to realize that their taunting words didn't matter. I could visualize the leader of the pack years later, living in his mom's basement, paying child support for two kids by two different mothers, one of whom would probably be a stripper. I didn't envy him anymore, and I most certainly didn't want to hang with his crew.

I wanted to be somebody.

XVI - Learning Curves

❧

Some chapters are meant to close. I went through the McDonald's management training program and learned techniques that I never dreamed of for dealing with people. I came to understand the necessity for policies and procedures that had baffled me as a base-level employee. I was introduced to the frankly daunting logistical and financial aspects of running a restaurant. It was an orgy of learning.

And I also enjoyed my work as a shift manager, keeping the restaurant running as smoothly as possible when I was in charge. I did my best to be a compassionate and positive manager, and nearly every day I learned valuable front-line lessons dealing with my people. I didn't always get as much respect as I had hoped for in my dreams of becoming a manager, but I went to work and came home each day with self-respect.

Those Golden Arches in my bedroom became more than a symbol of opportunity; they became a symbol of my success. Ironically, my new job also fed my drive to succeed and my curiosity to discover what else I might accomplish. My English was slowly improving and so was my self-confidence, so I decided to take a chance and start applying for better jobs.

At the same time, I knew that a solid education was the foundation for success, so after my high school graduation I applied to Eastern Michigan University. It was not only a fine school; it was inexpensive and close to home. I wasn't a typical student, though. I wasn't going to football games or hanging out at the student commons area. In order to pay for the education I wanted, I had to take the best job I could get and work as hard as I could work.

During my freshman year I landed a job as an assistant manager of a discount tire store. To schedule around my classes I worked early mornings and late nights, and I had to supervise employees whose work ethic was so bad that some of them would arrive at work intoxicated. Before long my fingers were grease-stained and my muscles ached from the effort of lifting more than my weight over and over again all day long. I was working through another frigid Michigan winter, and I thought that my bones would give out.

My parents had sacrificed everything for my chance to make something of myself, so if I had to work myself nearly to death while attending college classes, then that's what I would do. No matter what, I had it in my mind to finish college, for my parents as much as for myself, to thank them for all the things they had given up for me to have a better life. It wasn't easy, and at times I wondered where all the hard work would lead me, but I remained steadfast in my dedication to doing the best I could do with whatever came my way.

After a while I became restless again. Heeding my mother's advice, I started looking for a white-collar job with more promise, and moved to part-time student status. By the time I was a sophomore, I wanted to move up, not just keep running in circles.

It's amazing when I think back to how easily I could have missed out on an opportunity of a lifetime. Every day as I walked down the streets of downtown Ann Arbor, I would pass by the TCF Bank building. I would see the men and women dressed for business, their shoes polished and wearing fine suits and dresses as if they had just walked out of Neiman Marcus. I began to imagine how great their lives must be.

Although my family and I were not living on bananas any longer, we weren't exactly rolling in cash either. I was grateful for what I had, but I knew that I wanted something better for my family. It was frustrating at times, because no matter where I worked or how hard I worked, I never seemed to get ahead.

And then I would pass by that bank building and daydream about what life would be like if only I had the chance to enter that world.

I didn't expect much when I filled out the lengthy TCF application, but as always I hoped for the best. Even though I squeezed the pen hard, the sweat from my hand caused a slight shift every time I pressed down on the paper. It may have been my imagination, but I felt like all the eyes in the waiting room were on me, more condemning than anyone at McDonald's.

The condemnation may have come from the fact that I was the only applicant who had come there in flip-flops and a t-shirt. At the time I didn't know any better than to dress like that, maybe expecting the bank to provide a uniform or a suit to wear on the job. I had never really thought about it. In any case, as I hunched over my application I tried to slide my flip-flops underneath the chair as far back as they'd go, to hide them from the world.

When I was finished, I asked to see the hiring manager, so I could personally hand deliver my application. After I handed it to him and started to walk away, I looked back to see that he was holding my application and looking me over carefully, head to toe.

On my way out the door, I inhaled the bank's definitive smell and envisioned being the one with the corner office, answering important calls and delegating important tasks. I thought about what it might feel like to make my way through the big bank, greeting everyone on my way to my own desk, with an engraved plaque on it that said Daniel Milstein. I felt a rush of hope because it all felt so close I could taste it.

Later that week, I got a call for an interview.

Since I didn't own the proper clothing for a bank interview, I felt from the start like I might be courting disaster, but when I got there I tried to stay calm and collected. I sat across the desk from the hiring manager in my t-shirt, jeans and flip-flops, and focused all my attention on understanding the questions the he asked me. I concentrated even harder on the pronunciation of each of my English words when I replied. The hiring manager must have been impressed with my answers, because he offered me the job on the spot.

When I returned home with the news, my parents were ecstatic, my brother was awe-struck, and I was sick with fear. It occurred to me that there had to be more to working in the bank than simply walking around the lobby in a suit and that I had no idea just what that would be. I was certain that I would not need my knowledge of the ideal temperature for French fries.

As for the suit, I knew that I would have to invest in a proper outfit for a banker. I went shopping and spent $2 at the Salvation Army for a pre-worn suit and tie that smelled of mildew and memories. My mother washed the scent out of the fibers, but I couldn't help wondering who'd worn that suit before me, and if it meant as much to him as it did to me.

Getting dressed for my first day of work, I was grateful that this manifestation of my dream was coming to light. From Golden Arches to pin-stripes, I felt that I was on my way. Now that I had a job that offered more money, more security, and room for advancement, I could do anything.

To this day, I'll never know why he hired me. Why, when there were more qualified applicants with a greater command of the English language, some of them with actual banking experience, would he take a chance on a young Ukrainian upstart? Maybe it was my passion, or maybe he recognized a little bit of himself in me. Maybe it was my grandfather's presence. Whatever it was, I had to pinch myself to believe it was happening.

My first week at TCF Bank in the Consumer Lending Department was not the fantasy job I had dreamed of. Most of the employees weren't very welcoming to the new guy. I would get long stares and strange looks, but no one offered the friendly hello or helpful advice that could have eased my nerves. I brushed it all off and kept a smile on my face, because I was there to work. If I made any new friends in the process, that would be a bonus.

In those first days, I didn't know what to expect of such a big job. In my orientation they explained that I would be processing home equity loan applications, and I didn't even know what that was. But even though I had a lot to learn, I felt confident that I could do the job, and I was ready for the challenge. The learning curve was tough because I had to interact with customers regularly, all the while working diligently to perfect my English so they would take me seriously.

Whenever I was speaking to someone, I would repeat what I'd just said, spelling it out more clearly. A lot of people took this the wrong way, thinking that I was being sarcastic, but I was simply trying to make sure they understood me. Anything that involves money puts people on edge, so I made it my goal to take the edge off and let the customer feel as if they were talking to an old friend.

Some of my fellow employees mistook my dedication to hard work as a threat. Some even found miniscule imperfections in my work and reported them directly to management in an attempt to get me into trouble. They must have seen the burning desire in my eyes to be the best man I could be. What they didn't realize is that I wasn't competing with them; I was competing with myself.

As diligently as I worked in those early days, there wasn't a moment that I wasn't looking over my shoulder, afraid that something could go wrong with my dream, or that I might get fired at any second.

But my manager had other plans, because he apparently recognized something in me. One day he asked me to come into his office because he had something important to tell me. I walked into his office fearing the worst, only to have him tell me that he was going to be transferring me to the sales department.

I didn't know it then, but this transfer was the key that would unlock the door to my ultimate success.

The next day I began training for the sales team. I heard whispers all through the office from those wondering why I deserved to be promoted while they weren't, but I kept my focus on the job. As the whispers swept through the bank, I kept to myself and vowed to work even harder just to prove them all wrong about me. If they'd have taken the time to get to know me, they'd have found a good man looking to provide for his family, not the hotshot new guy they pinned me as.

I was hungry to learn and improve. I tried to do things in a way that would get the best results for the bank and to make me stand out. I was one of the first employees in every morning and one of the last to leave every night. I worked smart, I aimed high, and I never lost sight of my grandfather's dream or the significance of those Golden Arches painted above my bed.

This is why I outsold everyone in the region in my first ninety days, became a top producer, and was promoted to assistant consumer lending manager at TCF Bank.

XVII - Proud to Be an American

࿔

T here is no way for a natural-born American to really understand the feeling of becoming a citizen.

For five years my family had been without a country. We gave up our USSR passports and citizenship when we committed to leaving, and from that moment on we were vulnerable, naked and unprotected by the Soviet government. In fact, we had no protection from the government itself. And while we never felt so physically threatened in America, we were still officially outsiders here.

So one evening in 1996, when my father gathered us in the kitchen and told us that we had met the five-year waiting period and could begin the citizenship process, I was a bit surprised at how excited I was.

It's funny the things that come to mind at a time like that. In high school we had read about President John F. Kennedy's famous inaugural address to the nation in 1961. He said, "And so, my fellow Americans: ask not what your country can do for you – ask what you can do for your country."

I thought, OK, now I'm going to be a "fellow American!" What can somebody like me do for my country?

Then it came to me that I already was doing it. I had met a number of other Russians through my work at the bank, families who were enduring many of the same struggles as my family and I had. One of the things about my job I enjoyed most was being in a position to help these people out. I could help them break the language barrier, and I could provide them with the bank's products; products that could improve their lives. Of course it certainly didn't hurt my sales figures, either.

I also found myself going a bit further and helping them get established, find an apartment, or buy a car. After all, there had been people there to reach out to us when we first arrived here, people whose generosity gave us the chance to survive. In a sense, we were all members of a "community," there to help each other.

So we filled out our applications, and then began to study for the challenging written test we would have to take about American history and culture.

For weeks I would come home from work each night and we would sit around the kitchen table quizzing each other: "Who was the 12th president?" "Name three people who signed the Declaration of Independence." At the time, these seemed to be difficult questions, and I suspect that many natural born citizens would not be able to answer many of them.

As I studied for my test, I thought back to school in Kiev. In the USSR, the government carefully controlled everything we were taught. The version of history we saw was always the Soviet version. They even tried to control our beliefs. Reading the U. S. Constitution, I realized that the First Amendment changed all that:

Congress shall make no law respecting an establishment of religion, or prohibiting the free exercise thereof; or abridging the freedom of speech, or of the press; or the right of the people peaceably to assemble, and to petition the Government for a redress of grievances.

This simple sentence means that our life in America is in many ways the exact opposite of life in the USSR. There, our only religion was the

State. We could not discuss politics or express our opinions without fearing government persecution.

In America, we are free to worship any way we please, or not at all. We are free to say what we believe without any fear of government reprisal. We can turn on the television and find out what is happening without listening to *Swan Lake*. All this established by one simple sentence!

Because of her age, my grandmother would not have been required to take the exam, but she insisted on joining us. As we all drove together to the Federal Building in Detroit, she nearly wept as she explained to me that becoming a citizen would be one of the highlights of her entire life.

A few weeks later, we learned that we had all passed our tests. On June 5, 1997 my family went to the Detroit courthouse to be sworn in as American citizens. There we stood side-by-side with a large group of people of other ages and nationalities. The judge asked us to raise our right hands and repeat the Pledge of Allegiance.

I looked around the room and saw that virtually all of us had tears in our eyes. I stood with these other new Americans and said proudly, "I pledge allegiance, to the flag...." Then we sang the national anthem. It was a brief and simple ceremony, yet it was incredibly meaningful to a roomful of people who had come to America by choice.

With the echo of the words, "… and the home of the brave" still hanging in the air, I looked around at my fellow new American citizens. Most of us simply stood there for a few seconds, trying to absorb the moment. Then we all burst into smiles and expressions of congratulations, shook hands, and clapped each other on the back.

I thought to myself, only in America.

XVIII - The Important Things

৵৵ঔ

There are moments in life you never forget. These moments are so powerful that they are life defining, career defining, and even self-defining. But sometimes these moments are so subtle and soft, barely the whisper of a feather across your cheek, that you don't notice them when they're happening. And sometimes these moments come in the form of a special person who changes your life so dramatically that when you look back, you realize that you would not be where you are – or who you are – without them.

For me that person was Gail Owen. Though I didn't realize it at the time, she helped mold me into who I am. Her presence caused a ripple that would affect me so deeply, so profoundly, that I feel its effects even today.

I was 22-years-old, I had nearly stalled in my progress toward my college degree, and I was hell-bent on moving up in my career. My sights were always set on the biggest fish. I was no longer completely broke, slowly inching my way out of American poverty, and climbing out of the depths of despair to make my way up the corporate ladder. This was my idea of the American dream, and I was determined to live it.

I had discovered that I had a knack for sales, and I was quickly promoted at TCF. I had a talent for influencing people, for putting them at ease, and for closing the sale.

To me, closing sales was more than gratifying. I was on a constant high. Even today, though my transactions are much larger than they were during that time, to close a deal gives me the same "walk through heaven" feeling. There is almost nothing better.

I was young and ambitious, and I was working hard and making good money for my employer. But at the end of the week I was just taking home a fixed salary. I wasn't exactly starving, but it was also clear that at this rate I would never get rich.

Looking around the industry, I began to realize that any really good salesperson could make big money on commissions. I made a few phone calls to some of my business contacts and almost immediately secured an offer for a commission-only job as a loan officer. I figured that if I were to collect commissions on even half the business I had been processing at the bank, I would be on my way, so I jumped.

If you try to land a plane before you build the runway, your landing can be pretty hard. I didn't have the industry knowledge or contacts to bring in immediate sales, and I didn't have any sort of guarantee to tide me over until I could build up a customer base.

No runway.

Still smarting from my first failure in the banking industry, I dusted myself off and took a job at Comerica Bank where I became a branch manager. It wasn't long, though, before I was getting impatient again, and decided to take another leap into sales. I still didn't have the knowledge I needed to succeed, and again I came down hard.

I realized that for what I wanted to accomplish, I would have to build a thorough understanding of the operational side of the banking industry. I went to InterFirst, a division of ABN Amro Bank, and willingly took less pay than I had been making as a branch manager to become an underwriter.

Working as an underwriter gave me a whole new understanding of the banking industry.

Knowledge is power, and I was gaining more knowledge every day. I knew that my move had been a good one. Yet at the same time something was missing. I was hungry.

Oh, my belly was full, and my refrigerator now was filled with more than bananas and bologna, but I was far from satisfied. I had dreams of bigger things, things I still wanted to do, and places I still wanted to go.

I was hungry for success.

It was not enough that I had a decent suit and a serviceable car - I wanted a tailored suit and the finest car. It was not enough that I had a nice place to live – I wanted to live in a place people would tell their friends about.

I wanted a suit and a car and a home that people in Kiev could tell their friends about. I wanted them to somehow know that Daniel Milstein, the little Jewish boy from the 5th floor, was more than they ever could have imagined.

So I talked a million miles a second. I moved like I was hooked on caffeine, and I never stayed still long enough to enjoy any of my successes. I was always onto the next thing. And the harder I worked, the more I rose in the company, and the more deals I closed.

But it still just wasn't enough. I felt empty.

And then one day I received a call from Gail, who with her husband Joe owned Golden Rule Mortgage, a fair-sized mortgage company based in Tampa, Florida. At the time I was still an underwriter at InterFirst, and she was calling me because I was working on one of her "problem" loans. She wanted to see if we could clear up the issues and get a closing.

It was a call that would change my life forever.

Many loan officers I had dealt with in the past were rude and short-tempered, and they seemed to view the relationship between loan officers on the sales side and underwriters on the operations side as some sort of winner-take-all combat.

Gail was different. I don't know what it was about her, but she was able to establish an instant connection with me. She was soft-spoken and polite, and had a way of getting under my skin (in a good way), directing every conversation right to the heart of matters. We soon found ourselves talking day and night, and I found myself sharing some of my most intimate goals and dreams with her. I told her about my feelings of unrest, and that I wished I could get back into sales where my heart was.

That's when she offered me the opportunity to come work for Golden Rule by opening an office in Michigan. Golden Rule was a family-owned mortgage company based in Tampa, Florida and although moving to tropical weather would have been appealing, I couldn't imagine breaking away from my family at that time. Opening an Ann Arbor branch was the perfect opportunity for me.

As we worked together, Gail became one of my dearest friends. In many ways she reminded me of my mother – nurturing, sweet, and unpretentious. She was quietly, modestly good at her job. She simply did what she needed to do, and she had a way of getting people to do what she needed them to do without pushing them.

This was strange to me. Having grown up in the Soviet Union, I had always considered brute force the best way to get what you wanted. Gail showed me by example that there was another way. She treated each of her clients like a family member no matter where they were from. You could never tell if she was talking on the phone to a long lost relative or a potential client; she was just Gail. Her method seemed counter-intuitive to me, yet it didn't take long for her ways to seep into my work habits.

She also taught me, figuratively, to "chew my food"; to slow down in life, enjoy it, and take my time. I was beginning to realize that nearly everything I had ever taught myself was not quite right.

The more time I spent with Gail and her family, the more they became like an actual family to me. Although over the next three years I only made two or three visits to Florida, I began to think of her son as a brother, and her husband Joe as a father.

I now know that these people have a great deal to do with who I am today. I owe my success as much to them as I do to my natural born family, and for that I am truly grateful.

I may have a natural talent for sales, but I had been missing the human touch. The gaps that I thought were only subtle and small were in reality the size of the Grand Canyon, and they had been costing me potential clients as well as the relationships that meant the most to me.

I quickly learned to stop being a know-it-all and to shut up and listen, and because of these lessons I eventually broke every single record in the company. I became so proficient under Gail's guidance that I became one of the top loan originators in the entire country.

During this time I reached another major milestone in my life. With my grandmother's unflagging encouragement, I transferred to Cleary University and finished my college degree.

During my commencement ceremony, I looked around at my fellow graduates and smiled to myself. Most of them were about to go to graduate school, to go on extended vacations, or to go out and start their new careers. I was already a successful mortgage banker, running my own division and earning nearly one million dollars a year.

Years later, for my 30th birthday party at a country club in front of over 200 people, Gail's husband Joe flew in to Michigan just so that he could grab the microphone and tell everyone how I had changed his and Gail's lives, allowing them to retire early.

All great things, they say, must come to an end. For all the important life lessons Gail and Joe taught me, I started to get that familiar itch and I knew that the time was near; that voice inside my head was telling me it was time to move on. But this time it was different. It was not about moving up in a company or searching for a greater opportunity in a bigger corporation. This was something else entirely.

I knew that I was going to have to tell Gail, my second mom, what I was thinking. I must have picked up the phone at least half a dozen times and rehearsed how I was going to tell her, unsure of how I would phrase it. How do you tell someone who gave you everything that you are moving on?

How I made it through that conversation, I don't know. But to my surprise, in her typical gentle, maternal way, Gail understood almost instantly and responded with class and grace, encouraging me to go for my dreams. She knew that I wasn't just going to transfer to another company this time. This time I was going to start my own business.

Part of me felt that forming a company was a dumb idea as soon as I heard myself say it. What was I thinking, leaving a cushy job with a guaranteed income at Golden Rule only to strike out on my own, where I would almost certainly stumble and fall? Excited as I was to have Gail's blessing and to jump at the opportunity, I still had this nagging feeling in the pit of my stomach.

Could I really do it on my own?

XIX - Saying Goodbye

᠅

"Can you go any faster?" I asked the taxi driver as I nervously drummed my fingers on my thigh.

"You want to drive while I sit in back and tell you how to do it?" he asked, his voice dripping with sarcasm.

I should have known better than to push a Russian taxi driver. I shook my head and stared out the window, listening to the slap of the car's windshield wipers as they battled the pounding summer rain.

My mind began to drift, to wander through memories of all that had happened over the last twenty years. I thought about all the triumphs, the failures, the joy, and the pain. There were so many things I wished I could do over again, and so many things I'm thankful I did.

The rain stopped, and the sun began to push its way through the clouds. Even though it had been so many years since I'd set foot in Kiev, I began to recognize familiar sights along the road.

The buildings had been cleaned up, restored, and stripped of the grey shroud that seemed to envelope so much of the USSR in my memory. The people on the streets seemed happy, and busy, and were well dressed. The sun gleamed on the domes of the churches, and from somewhere, maybe St. Sophia's, I could hear the bells ringing.

A sea of cars flowed around us, but they were not like the boxy, smoking Soviet cars we knew. They were BMWs, and Ladas, and Mercedes, even a Rolls Royce or two. And there were so many more cars than I could ever have imagined on these roads.

And then, as the cab came to the top of a hill I saw her, sword and shield held high, welcoming me back to Kiev: the Motherland Memorial. The sun burst over her, bathing her in the same magical glow I had seen with my father so many years ago.

I had flown to Kiev for a purpose, and as much as I was fascinated by the new look of my hometown, I was also nervous. I checked my Blackberry, hoping that responding to the flurry of emails would drown out my anxiety.

I was out of the cab almost before it pulled to a stop. Cemeteries weren't my favorite places, but this day and this cemetery were important to me.

As I walked among the tombstones, I couldn't help but wonder how my life would have turned out if we had not taken the risk to come to America, if we had stayed in Ukraine. What if we had been caught or betrayed? As I scanned the names on the tombstones, I wondered how many of these people had tried to make their lives better and failed.

And then I found myself, after twenty long years, once again standing at the grave of my grandfather.

They say that when you're dead, you're gone, but to me this man was still very much alive. Over all those years, every time things would get tough or I felt like giving up, I would hear his encouraging words echoing in my ear, as if he stood behind me with his hand on my shoulder.

Then, as I stood there clutching in my hand the one thing that I swore I would bring with me if I ever returned, the reality of the situation hit me hard. Suddenly I was that 12-year-old boy again, talking to my grandfather for what I believed to be the last time.

"I made it," I told him. "I came back to you. I didn't think I would ever be allowed back in the country to see you again, but I'm here, Grandpa. I know it's been a long time, much longer than I wanted it to be, but... Oh, Grandpa, I hope you'll forgive me."

I felt my throat tighten and tears well up in my eyes. Where could I begin? How do you tell someone who meant so much to you about your twenty-year adventure in a new world?

"Grandpa, I tried to remember everything you said," I began. "I tried to remember everything you taught me."

And then the tears ran down my cheeks as the words came spilling out of my mouth. I told him about walking the halls in a strange school in a strange land; about bananas and bologna; about French fries and the Golden Arches; about banking and underwriting; about the nights sleeping on the couch at my office; about the struggle to get my company off the ground when everyone told me it couldn't be done. The years of pain and struggle, the triumphs, the blessings, all came out faster than I could keep up with.

I don't remember half of what I said, but I have to think that somehow, my grandfather could hear me. As the breeze began to pick up and rustle the leaves on the trees around me I thought that maybe, in his own way, my grandfather was telling me it was all right. I began to smile.

"So it worked," I said. "I listened to everything you told me, and I worked harder than anybody else, and it worked.

"Can you believe it? Out of half a million people in the lending industry, I became the number one residential lender in the world. My company is the 42nd largest lender in the United States. I'm at the pinnacle of my career, and I'm only 36. I can hardly believe it myself. I've achieved things most people chase for their entire lives.

"I have more than 500 employees working for my company now, in 48 offices across the country. We have been named one of the *Inc.* 500 fastest growing companies in the United States. I've written a bestselling book, and I've been awarded an honorary doctorate.

"I've raised and donated millions of dollars to charity, and my company was voted one of the top workplaces in all of Michigan four years in a row. I've won a lot of awards, Grandpa, but that's the one that means the most to me. I have treated people right, just like you taught me. I must have done something right because..."

My voice trailed off. I knew that my grandfather would be proud of all my material accomplishments, but I also knew that these were not the things that would really matter the most to him. A new smile spread across my face as I thought about the one thing he would have asked me, the one thing he would have really cared about.

"Yes, Grandpa, I am happy. And I'm a daddy now," I told him. "Her name is Julie. She's 10-years old and she has your eyes. She has your spirit."

The taxi driver leaned on his horn, gunning his engine to show me how displeased he was that I was taking so long. I knew it was time to go. I had said what I needed to say and I had done what I needed to do.

I laid a copy of my book, *The ABC of Sales*, at his grave, along with some fresh flowers, kissed his stone and said, "Hope you're proud of me, Grandpa. Goodbye."

XX - Home

࿇

It was good to be home – in America. As I stepped into my parents' newly remodeled home, I embraced my mother and father and thought about how much I valued them. My daughter Julie had been staying with them for the last five days, and it felt like a lifetime since I'd seen my little girl. I pulled her close to me and inhaled her aroma, the scent of candy, soap, and innocence that always warmed my heart. She ran off and gathered her things as I sat down with my mother and father for a chat.

We talked about what it was like after all those years to finally return to Kiev, to see my grandfather's grave. We talked about what I said, what I didn't say, and what they wished I could have said. They wanted to know if I told my grandfather about how my brother Alex had become one of the most prominent realtors in Michigan. My trip back wasn't just for me: it was for all of us.

I caught my mom and dad looking at me in my custom-tailored suit with a twinkle in their eyes. They said nothing, but their expressions spoke volumes. As loving and caring as my parents always have been, it's just not the Russian way to shower anyone with compliments. You always look forward, and you never look back.

But just before I stepped out the door, I had to say one thing: "I'm not sure I've ever taken the time to say this, but thank you. Thank you for everything."

How do you put into words the gratitude you have for two people who put their lives on hold, who scraped and saved and slaved away so that their children could have a better life? I only hoped that they knew what I was trying to express, and judging by the tears in my mother's eyes, I believe they did.

As we walked out the door, Julie began to jump up and down, proclaiming just how hungry she was. I looked into my daughter's eyes. September 7th - her birthday - was the best day of my life, I thought to myself. She squeezed my hand as we walked together down the walk from my parents' doorstep.

At the car she stopped, wrapped her arms around me and held on tight. My daughter completes me in a way that nothing else ever has. When I was building my business, I would always work nonstop when she was asleep or at school, just to make sure I could spend every spare second with her when she was awake. I vowed to never let work interfere with my time with my baby. I went to every school event and every meeting. I picked her up every day and took her to school myself. There was no sacrifice I could make for her that would be too much. The mere thought of her made me want to be a better man.

Right before little Julie was born, I remember praying that she would come on a Friday night so I wouldn't have to take any time off work. I didn't realize how much my life was about to change. I had been working so hard to grow my business that I had no idea how different things would be with a little one to take care of.

It didn't matter that I worked 6 AM to 10 PM every day. I got up with her in the night, changed her diapers, fed her, and watched her grow. Over the years the long hours and hard work might have helped destroy my marriage to Julie's mother, but they never came between my daughter and me. Even now, I still help with her homework and tuck her into bed every night.

There were many nights when I'd take a break from work at 1:00 a.m. just to go watch her sleep. Her face was like an angel; peaceful and perfect. I could hardly believe that I could be so blessed. It made my heart hurt just thinking of a day without her. There is nothing more important than her.

Nothing

"I'm hungry," she reminded me again, looking up at me. She pouted her lip out like a fish and pulled down on my hands.

As she hopped into the car and I made sure she buckled herself up, I realized that my stomach was growling too. A smile spread across my face as a thought occurred to me. I knew just where to take her, a place I hadn't been to in more than seventeen years.

It was about lunch hour as we drove through town, weaving through traffic while the enormous buildings towered over us. I parked the car and carefully helped Julie step out. We held hands and crossed the parking lot, making our way through the big double doors. The Golden Arches gave me a chill as all the old memories came flooding back.

We stood back for a moment, away from the McDonald's counter. I wasn't reading the menu that I knew by heart, I was studying the faces of people I had once worked with, those who were still working at McDonald's.

"Can I take your order?" one of them said, without looking up. My voice was strong as I placed our order. The man looked up at me with a start. He was older and a little grayer, but it was Roger, my former manager.

At first it seemed like he didn't recognize me, and there was a part of me that was glad about that. So many memories came to mind of those endless days, of my aching shoulders, and my grease-stained clothes. I could still smell the Pine Sol and bleach that stung my nostrils as I mopped the floors.

Roger stood clasping the top of his shirt collar with one sweaty hand, as if he was ashamed of the uniform he still wore. "Daniel, it's been a long time," he said. "How are you? Where are you working now?"

I cleared my throat. The line behind me was getting longer, as customers were waiting for us to order. I wondered if he was asking out of genuine interest, or if he hoped that I was not doing anything important. "I have a good job with Gold Star Financial," I said. His eyes lit up as if he was impressed, and he told me that he had heard it was a good company. I saw a bead of sweat from his forehead trailing down his cheek.

I ordered a Happy Meal for Julie and something for me, and when he gave me the total, the numbers on the register were somehow clearer than I had ever seen them. Looking from a different perspective, I felt grateful that I had been given the chance to work here, no matter how difficult it had been. I handed him the money, then reached over to shake his hand.

"Thank you so much for giving me the opportunity all those years ago."

He grabbed my hand and told me that I was one of the best he ever had, and that he was proud that I made something out of myself.

I looked down at Julie and realized that I really had come full circle with my past. I was overwhelmed with gratitude and the realization that I was an American citizen who had built my dream from the ground up, and that I really had made it.

I pulled a card from my pocket and placed it next to the cash register. "If you ever need anything Roger, anything, please give me a call."

He picked up the card and smiled, I think almost enjoying the irony of what was happening. I swear I could see his eyes starting to water as he nodded at me.

He handed me my change, and although at first I thought about putting it in my pocket, I looked at it, looked at my daughter, and handed it to her.

17 cents.

Julie smiled up at me and ran off to sit down. I wasn't much older than her when my grandfather first told me about America, when I began to think about all that could be possible if only I just believed. I had begun my journey with 17 cents, setting out on an adventure that turned out to be the best thing that could have ever have happened to me and my family. 17 cents was all it took – just 17 cents, and a dream.

As the teenager in his McDonald's uniform handed me my tray, I caught sight of a mop leaning against the wall back by the drive-thru. I thanked him and smiled to myself at how far I'd come in my life.

Not bad for a kid from Kiev.

Epilogue

☙❧

On June 2, 2012, a little more than twenty years after first setting foot in this country speaking not a word of English, I gave the commencement address to the new graduates of Cleary University. It was fifteen years, almost to the day, after reciting the Pledge of Allegiance during my American citizenship ceremony.

On this day the University also conferred on me, the proudest member of the Russian community in the midwest, an Honorary Doctorate. I stood at the podium and spotted my mom sitting in the front row with tears running down her cheeks. I smiled at the realization that I had become a Doctor for her after all.

This is the text of my speech:

Good morning.

Being up here today is deeply personal for me. Not only because I am able to share this with my family and friends, but also because it symbolizes a major milestone in the journey from another world and another life thousands of miles away.

I came to the United States as a teenager with just 17 cents in my pocket and one suitcase stuffed to the brim.

Most kids at that age are figuring out who to ask to the prom or how to save enough money to buy their first car. But my family and I were taking a huge risk, leaving everything we knew in the Soviet Union: family, friends, home, jobs, and even our very own way of life for the chance at something much greater.

On a cold December night in 1991, we arrived in America to a subsidized one-bedroom apartment. There were five of us.

We were living on food stamps. We did not speak English, or know any good places to get jobs. We had nothing besides the memories that we could carry in our suitcases, and in our pockets. All we had was the hope that once we took this gamble, our dreams would come true.

I have benefitted from the support of many teachers, mentors, work associates, and others. The wonderful thing about involving people in your dreams is that they also get to watch as you reach your big milestones. I can't tell you how proud my grandmother and parents were as they

watched me graduate from Cleary 10 years ago.
They were my biggest supporters along the way.

Today is a day of dreams fulfilled again – my
own, and yours.

As I travel around the country on speaking
engagements, I often hear recent graduates and
young professionals talk about some of the same
things that worried me when I moved to America.
They worry about getting jobs or starting their
own business. They say unemployment is too
high. Economic recessions, financial meltdowns,
and many other events will pose challenges too
difficult to overcome.

I know how bleak the path ahead can look,
but the bottom line is, you have to make your
dreams come true. No one else is going to do it
for you.

I would like to share a couple stories about
people facing challenges, and making their
dreams happen.

The first is about a businessman named
Amadeo Giannini who lived in the San Francisco
bay area in the early part of the 20th century. He
opened his business in an old saloon and catered
to the hardworking immigrants that others would
not serve at the time.

Shortly after Giannini set up shop, the Great
Earthquake struck in 1906. Homes were reduced

to rubble. Rather than leave the area as many did, he decided that he would help members of the area by lending them money, proclaiming, "San Francisco would be the first to rise from the ashes." Since most of the banks in the area had been destroyed and were unable to loan money, Giannini set up a plank across two barrels at the corner of an intersection. There he collected deposits, and made rebuilding loans to businesses based on a handshake.

He got the economy moving again.

Little did anyone know at the time that these loans and deposits would form the basis of the portfolio that would later become Bank of America, one of the largest financial institutions in the world.

He didn't invent commercial lending. But what he did do was take a fresh perspective on an old idea. He accomplished what others thought was impossible by not being afraid to dream big.

Yes, you have to balance dreams with reality. Always be careful of listening too closely to those who tell you your dreams are too wild, too impractical, and not possible.

Believe when most doubt...

Work when most play...

Win when most lose

Dream when most sleep...

Be focused when most are undecided

Let me tell you about a mortgage company founded by a young 24-year-old with a vision to provide the American Dream of homeownership. This company with only one employee opened its doors to the public 12 years ago in a tiny space that was used as a closet by its previous tenant. It had $3,000 in startup capital.

Seven years later, the worst financial meltdown in the history of the world occurred. Banks were paralyzed and stopped lending. The stock market crashed and unemployment was at the worst levels since the Great Depression. Many people were losing their jobs, their homes, and their life savings. Wall Street household names such as Bear Stearns and Lehman Brothers, along with thousands of other banks and lending institutions, were forced to shut down and seek protection under bankruptcy law. Mortgage giants Fannie Mae and Freddie Mac were seized by the government.

By that time, the founder was 31 years old with little less than 12 years' experience in the banking industry. His company now had 100 employees and two offices.

The financial meltdown required a major shift in his overall focus. More than ever, he felt responsibility to his employees, and many more spouses, children, and families who depended on his company's stability.

He was enjoying his very successful career, but the company's future was not about him. The overriding goal was preserving the jobs and the livelihood of his employees. When the global financial meltdown hit, he told his people that his mortgage company would not participate in the world recession.

At the time, many employees' family members were losing jobs daily.

This young president made a pledge to his people that no matter what happened, no one would lose their jobs—even if he had to infuse his own life savings to make the payroll.

Within six months over 60% of the industry competition closed their doors permanently. This company cleaned its balance sheet and never stopped lending.

It was their moment to shine.

By 2008, the company's revenues went up 712%. Over 200 new jobs were created and four new offices were opened. His business made the *Inc.* 500 list of the fastest growing companies in the United States.

This expansion was once again doubled the following year. In 2012, 12 years later, this company is the 42nd largest residential lender in the United States with over 500 associates in 43 offices across the country.

Today, not so young anymore, I stand in front of you wearing a cap and a gown as the founder and Chief Executive Officer of Gold Star Mortgage Financial Group.

I achieved my dreams thanks to my hard working co-workers and their dedication, but also because of Cleary University, which gave me the tools I needed to make my vision a reality.

Much like the 100-year-old story of Bank of America, the story of Gold Star Mortgage Financial Group is still being written.

A dream doesn't become reality through magic; it takes sweat, determination, and hard work.

As you begin your post-graduate journey, I think some great advice is to throw away the store-bought map and create your own pathway to achieve your dreams.

One of my hopes for you today is that you continue dreaming on a grand scale. Dream about being the top professional in your field, about starting your own company, or becoming a senator. Whatever you dream about, dream about being the best that you can possibly be.

The road will not always be easy. When you encounter setbacks or roadblocks, do not underestimate the power of determination and innovation.

Don't let failure stand in your way. Most successful people have failed on their way to achieving their goals. Henry Ford's early businesses failed and left him broke five times before he founded the iconic Ford Motor Company. As a young student, Thomas Edison was told by his teachers that he was "too stupid to learn anything" and his ideas too impractical. Of course, his invention illuminated the world.

Abraham Lincoln had numerous business failures, lost seven elections, and barely got 100 votes in his quest for the Vice Presidential nomination, before, finally, being elected as the 16th President of the United States.

I stumbled myself a couple of times before I earned success. Just as Henry Ford, Thomas Edison, Abraham Lincoln, and many others did. They had to experience it before they could be truly great.

Experience is always the hardest teacher, because it gives the exam first, and then teaches the lesson.

It is important to avoid "spending so much time trying to choose the perfect opportunity that you miss the right opportunity." Recognize that there will be failures, and acknowledge that there will be obstacles. There is very little learning in success. You must learn instead from your mistakes and the mistakes of others, and use innovation to overcome your obstacles.

Take Kenneth Cole for example, the famous designer, who faced many challenges starting his company. He wanted to showcase his new line of shoes during the fashion market week at the Hilton Hotel in New York. Not an easy thing to do. He could not afford to purchase a hotel room or showroom to exhibit his line, and wanted to sell them on the street instead.

The problem was that the only companies that could get street permits at the time were either utility companies or movie companies. So he changed his letterhead to "Kenneth Cole Productions" and went to city hall to apply for a permit to shoot a movie called "The Birth of a Shoe Company." They had a fully furnished forty-foot trailer, stage lights, a director, a rolling camera, and models as actresses. In two and a half days, they sold forty thousand pairs of shoes. To this day the formal name of the company remains "Kenneth Cole Productions," highlighting the importance of innovation and creativity.

Colin Powell once said, "There are no secrets to success. It is the result of preparation, hard work, and learning from failure."

Whether you have already found your calling today, or if you're still searching, your dreams should be what drive you to succeed.

As you accept your diploma today, think proudly of what you have accomplished and what you still have planned. I join your family members and friends in congratulating your achievement, and I wish you great success in your future!

Thank you very much.

About the Author

❧

Daniel Milstein is known as a successful business executive, author, job creator, company builder, entrepreneur, and founder and CEO of Gold Star Mortgage Financial Group, an *Inc.* 500 Company.

Born in Kiev, Ukraine, Dan and his family experienced hardship, religious persecution, and life-and-death situations, all in the shadows of one of the greatest disasters that ever occurred, the explosion at the Chernobyl nuclear plant.

Forced to escape the Soviet government, Dan's family fled to Ann Arbor, Michigan. Highly motivated to succeed, Dan worked his way up from mopping floors in a McDonald's restaurant, through a series of difficult and challenging jobs, to ultimately establish one of the 15 fastest-growing financial services companies in the United States.

He graduated with honors from Cleary University, earning a business degree, and was awarded an honorary Doctorate from his alma mater. He is currently in his second term on the Cleary University Board of Trustees.

Under Dan's leadership, Gold Star has grown to more than 500 employees in 48 offices across the U.S. The company has been named a Top Workplace in Michigan for four consecutive years by the *Detroit Free Press*, and a Michigan Economic Bright Spot by *Corp!* magazine.

Dan has been ranked the #1 loan officer in the United States, out of more than 550,000 professionals in the lending industry. He has been included in the prestigious "40 Under 40" in *Crain's* magazine, "30 in Their Thirties" in DBusiness magazine, and has been named one of the nation's 40 Top Finance Professionals by *National Mortgage Professional* magazine.

Dan is the author of *The ABC of Sales: Lessons from a Superstar*, which in March 2012 sold 10,000 copies and became the #1 sales book on Amazon.com. He is also a contributing writer for multiple business publications. As an author, he has earned numerous awards and honors at national and international book festivals in Paris, New York, Los Angeles, San Francisco, and New England.

In 2012, Milstein was named to the prestigious National Academy of Best-Selling Authors.

Acknowledgments

❧❧

This book would not have been possible without the guidance and support of some very special people to me. I'd like to personally thank my family who has shared this journey with me, and whom without their patience and strength, I would not be where I am today. I'd also like to thank Mike, Candace, Jeff, David and Scott for their editorial, marketing, and publicity guidance from the beginning. You helped me crystallize my words so that I could share them with the world. To Mark Victor Hansen who generously wrote the foreword to my memoir and whose encouragement along the way has been invaluable. To Gail & Joe Owen and my second family at Gold Star Financial who have helped make so many of my dreams come true. I'd also like to thank my many friends and coworkers, too many to name, (you know who you are) who I subjected to the reading of earlier drafts of this book, and who gave me honest feedback so that I could polish this into the most heartfelt story that I could tell. And last but not least, to Kelly who went over every page, every sentence with a fine-toothed comb and whose wisdom and feedback were insurmountable.

Index

⤜❦⤛

A

B

C

D

Here's What People Are Saying About
17 Cents and a Dream

"Through pure determination, fortitude and attitude, Daniel pulled out of impossibly difficult situations. His story is true, his story is a personal inspiration to me and I hope it will inspire you too to maximize your potential and go for the greatest of dreams."

Mark Victor Hansen
Bestselling Author, *Chicken Soup for the Soul*

"Powerful and inspiring, Daniel Milstein's story is a testament to following your dreams and never taking no for an answer."

Seth Green
Actor, Writer/Director *Adult Swim*

"Dan Milstein shows that the American Dream is alive and well for everyone, immigrant and natural born citizen alike."

Ross Rojek
San Francisco/Sacramento Book Review

"Dan Milstein is living the American Dream with his incredible real-life rags to riches story of coming to this country with only pennies in his pocket and becoming a wildly successful businessman. As impressive is his love for American ideals and making a difference in the community. A must read for anyone wanting to be inspired!"

Carol Cain
Emmy winning producer/host CBS' "Michigan Matters" and *Detroit Free Press* columnist

"This is what the American dream is all about.
From McDonald's to millionaire.
From dream to reality."

Jess Todtfeld
Former FOX-TV Producer
President, Success In Media, Inc.

"Especially during this time of financial strain and pessimism this beautifully written memoir serves as food for the soul. Reading this book not only is an engrossing experience – it is an uplifting one. As Milstein would encourage us, believe, and struggle even, because anything is possible if we truly remember the American Dream."

Grady Harp
Amazon Top Ten Reviewer – 5 Stars

"Dan Milstein's journey from Kiev to where he is today is a remarkable story. In such as short amount of time he's built a great company while maintaining a sterling reputation."

John W. Barfield
Founder, Bartech Group

"17 Cents and a Dream proves that the only limitations in life exist in one's own mind. Dan Milstein's book is a testimony to the fact that if one remains steadfast and determined, as well as faithful, they can exceed even their own greatest expectations."

Zane
26-time New York Times bestselling author

"With his mesmerizing *17 Cents and a Dream*, Daniel Milstein delivers more than the usual rags to riches memoir. It is rather a riveting and spellbinding testimony that with the right combination of motivation and perseverance daunting challenges and appalling events can be overcome no matter what the odds may be against you."

Norm Goldman
Publisher & Editor of Bookpleasures.com

"Dan Milstein's is the classic story of a young Russian immigrant achieving the American dream against all odds. It is a great personal story, a great Jewish story and a great story of how immigrants continue to help build America."

David Shtulman
Jewish Federation of Greater Ann Arbor

"As a supplier of fine food for restaurants and grocers I know the main ingredient to success is hard work and the willingness to go above and beyond the customer's expectations to deliver satisfaction. Dan Milstein demonstrates this principal in many ways. As an entrepreneur I can appreciate his struggles, hopes and aspirations. This book is an inspiration as it proves that in America anything is possible."

Jim Lipari
Lipari Foods

Watch for the second half of Daniel Milstein's inspiring story, and for more Superstar sales techniques, in two new books,

Coming Soon!

15311709R10113

Made in the USA
San Bernardino, CA
22 September 2014